Political Culture

Basic Concepts in Political Science

William A. Welsh, GENERAL EDITOR

STUDYING POLITICS, William A. Welsh, *University of Iowa*

SOCIALIZATION TO POLITICS, Dean Jaros, *University of Kentucky*

PUBLIC POLICY-MAKING, James E. Anderson, *University of Houston*

POLITICAL CULTURE, Walter A. Rosenbaum, *University of Florida*

MANAGING POLITICAL CONFLICT, Dennis Pirages,
University of California, San Diego

Political Culture

WALTER A. ROSENBAUM

PRAEGER PUBLISHERS
New York

Selections from Gabriel A. Almond and Sidney Verba, *The Civic Culture: Political Attitudes and Democracy in Five Nations* (copyright © 1963 by Princeton University Press), pp. 9–10, 17–18, 19, 22, 102, and 267. Reprinted by permission of Princeton University Press.

Tables from Donald J. Devine, *The Political Culture of the United States,* pp. 100, 148. Copyright © 1972 by Little, Brown and Company (Inc.). Reprinted by permission.

Published in the United States of America in 1975
by Praeger Publishers, Inc.
111 Fourth Avenue, New York, N.Y. 10003

© 1975 by Praeger Publishers, Inc.

Library of Congress Cataloging in Publication Data

Rosenbaum, Walter A
   Political culture.

   Bibliography: p.
   Includes index.
   1. Political sociology.   2. Political psychology.
I. Title.
JA76.R65   301.5′92   73-10917
ISBN 0-275-19620-8
ISBN 0-275-85200-8 pbk.

Printed in the United States of America

CONTENTS

SERIES EDITOR'S INTRODUCTION

This book is one of a series of volumes, published and forthcoming, written for introductory and intermediate undergraduate courses in political science. In one sense, the purpose of these books is to introduce students to the field of political science. The core volume in the series, *Studying Politics*, presents an overview of the concepts, approaches, and subject matter of the discipline, together with an introduction to elements of critical thinking about the study of politics. Each of the other volumes in the series focuses on one or two central concepts used to describe major areas of political activity. These concept volumes provide definitions of important terms, summarize basic approaches, and describe what political scientists have discovered about the involvement of human beings in these activities—political socialization, the exercise of power and influence, conflict, policy-making, political leadership, the development of political culture, the formation and activities of political groups. By using various combinations of these relatively short books, instructors can structure, as broadly or as selectively as they wish, an introduction to the study of politics for undergraduate students.

In another sense, the purpose of this series is both less "academic" and more ambitious. For this series proceeds from the premise that what political scientists do *qua* political scientists has relevance well beyond the relatively narrow confines of a scholarly discipline. As political science has labored toward greater precision, rigor, and theoretical maturity, it has developed new ways of organizing and studying information about politics. By now, there is substantial agreement that these new approaches and techniques have—on balance—improved the scientific status of the discipline. But what of those who are not committed to becoming professional political scientists, but who nevertheless seek a sound, reliable understanding of politics, simply because political activity is so central to the management of human affairs? Does the development of systematic perspectives in the field of political science contribute only to the advancement of science, yielding no benefits for the thoughtful layman?

If one of the goals of science is to provide understanding of our environment, then scientists and nonscientists alike surely share that concern. If this is the case, then our progress as political scientists should hold the promise of improved understanding for nonscientists as well. In short, what political scientists have learned about how to study politics—especially about the close relationship between *what* we know and *how* we find out—ought to be useful to anyone who wants to understand politics. That belief constitutes the principal motivation for this series of books.

In pursuit of that goal, these books attempt to do four things. First, they introduce students to the language and approaches of political science—not merely as elements of a scholarly discipline, but as useful ways of looking at the world we live in. Second, relatedly, these books raise some basic methodological issues involved in studying politics—not as abstract issues in scholarship but as problems of how we obtain and critically analyze information available to us. Third, the concept-based volumes in this series introduce the student to concrete aspects of political activity through the use of unifying concepts that cut across both traditional subfields of the discipline and formal institutions, or structures, of government. They treat politics as a blend of several types of human behavior. Fourth, the books in the series attempt to overcome the student's natural parochialism—the limitations imposed by his much greater familiarity with the political practices and structures of the society in which he lives—by providing frequent examples of political activity from a variety of cultural settings. In short, the series seeks to be both systematic and concrete. It is designed to provide useful perspectives on an exciting area of human activity, and to present these perspectives in a way that is meaningful for students who are beginning their formal study of the subject.

The task is ambitious, and the accomplishment doubtless will be less than perfect. But the effort seems worthwhile, if we hope to establish the relevance of the discipline of political science not only to theory-building in social science but also to sound, reliable understanding of politics on the part of concerned citizens.

WILLIAM A. WELSH

Political Culture

THE MEANING OF
POLITICAL CULTURE

A fragmentation grenade explodes inside a crowded Catholic pub in Northern Ireland, shredding the air with shrapnel, killing four people, and adding another vicious episode to a civil war between Protestants and Catholics that has already claimed more than a thousand victims in that violence-racked land. Far away, a Montreal housewife removes from a supermarket shelf a ketchup bottle with a unique label, a modest symbol of crisis averted. Found only in Canada, the label bears French and English wording of equal size proclaiming "ketchup" and *"ketchup aux tomates"*; repealing the law requiring such bilingual labels would produce a parliamentary crisis. To Canada's south, an opinion poll declares that the American public, apparently shaken by continuing revelations of scandal within the executive branch, is losing confidence in the Presidency—a scant 19 per cent of the public express strong faith in that institution. Still, the American people do not seem moved to demand any radical alterations in their political system.

Such provocative items, chosen from one day's news, are likely to prompt the question "Why?" Why cannot Catholics and Protestants in Northern Ireland reach a political accommodation without civil war? Why is language a politically explosive issue in Canada? Why do Americans express low confidence in their Chief Executive yet remain curiously undemonstrative in the sort of situation that has provoked political violence in other nations? Here—in our effort to understand both the commonplace and the extraordinary in political life—the study of *political culture* properly begins. The concept of political culture offers a potentially powerful, and almost always useful, approach to daily political events by identifying the underlying psychological forces that shape much of civic life.

Political culture can be defined in two ways, depending upon the level at which we want to study political life. If we concentrate on the individual, political culture has a basically psychological focus. It entails all the important ways in which a person is subjectively oriented toward the essential elements in his political system.[1] We want to know what he feels and thinks about the symbols, institutions, and rules that constitute the fundamental political order of his society and how he responds to them. In effect, we are probing the psychological dimension of a person's civic life; we ask what bonds exist between him and the essentials of his political system and how these bonds affect his behavior.

The second definition of political culture refers to the collective orientation of people toward the basic elements in their political system. This is a "system level" approach. We are interested in how large masses of citizens evaluate their political institutions and officials. To say, for example, that a nation's political culture is largely "integrated" means that most people within the system have similar, or compatible, political culture orientations, which are congenial to the political institutions within which they live. When political culture is discussed, it usually refers to these mass political orientations across the whole political system.

Before sharpening this definition, I can briefly illustrate how an awareness of political culture enhances our understanding of the political events we described above. Northern Ireland's violence, for example, flows in part from the widespread conviction among the Catholic minority that the government is illegitimate and in part from the profound distrust of each other's religious communities that permeates the Catholic and Protestant factions alike, frustrating political accommodation and moderation. In short, one must know something about public attitudes toward government and toward other political factions before explaining the civil war. In a similar vein, Canada's official bilingualism is comprehensible only when we note the importance that the large

French minority attaches to its language and culture; its conviction that it is struggling for cultural survival against the English majority, and its determination, forces official governmental recognition of its cultural demands, even to the level of ketchup bottles. Finally, Americans have traditionally held their Constitution in high esteem, believing that the government it designed is legitimate and proper; moreover, there is broad public conviction that political change should be orderly and peaceful, following the customary means ordained by the Constitution. Undoubtedly, this sentiment keeps most citizens loyal to their basic governmental system and wary of radical or violent change. They may have been disillusioned with President Nixon but not disposed to demand major refashioning of the Presidency; they may criticize Congress or the Court, but they are not yet prepared to redesign either institution. There are, to be sure, no simple, all-inclusive explanations for complex political events; political culture never explains all. Still, a sensitivity to the perspective it provides on political life adds depth and richness to our appreciation of political events.

The Essentials of Political Culture

To say that political culture involves the important ways in which people are subjectively oriented toward the basic elements of their political system is an accurate but not yet satisfactory definition. One needs a firmer notion of what "subjective orientations" this involves and, consequently, we need to spell out, clearly and concretely, the distinctive elements of thought, feeling, and behavior that concern us. At this point a nettlesome issue arises. Scholars themselves have never reached a consensus on the proper components of political culture; so many different formulations have been offered (twenty-five by one count) that one might think he was grappling with the riddle of the Sphinx. At one extreme, some analysts include in political culture "all politically relevant orientations either of a cognitive, evaluative or expressive sort"—so unbounded a definition that an investigator would have to spend an interminable time compiling an elephantine list of orientations to be sure nothing *politically relevant* escaped notice.[2] At the other extreme, certain analysts attempt to make the list manageable by limiting political culture to orientations toward national political institutions, a good beginning except that it may omit other dimensions of political life very instrumental in shaping the fundamental political order of a society.³ Fortunately, this profusion of definitions need not mean intellectual anarchy, for one can distill from them a set of common items most scholars would agree belong among the essentials; we shall call these the "core components" of political culture.

The Core Components. What the core elements appear to share is a fundamental importance in shaping a nation's political order. Whenever analysts offer such a list they are, in effect, using a rule of thumb: Those dimensions of an individual's thoughts, feelings, or behaviors that are linked to the creation and maintenance of a society's fundamental political order belong under the label "political culture." Thus, insists one observer, political culture must be limited to the "attitudes, beliefs and sentiments that give order and meaning to the political process and provide the underlying assumptions and rules that govern behavior."⁴

It is helpful to think of these core components as orientations toward different elements in the political order. Such a list commonly includes the following particulars:

1. *Orientations Toward Governmental Structures*
   a. *Regime Orientation*—How an individual evaluates and responds to the basic governmental institutions of his society, its symbols, officials, and norms (collectively, the "regime"); this may include a more detailed investigation of orientations toward specific institutions and offices or an investigation of preferences for alternative governmental structures.
   b. *Orientations Toward Governmental Inputs and Outputs*—How individuals feel and respond toward various demands for public policy ("inputs") and policy decisions made by government ("outputs"); this may include an inventory of a person's knowledge concerning how these processes operate, what demands he may make upon government, and how effective he believes governmental policy to be.

2. *Orientations Toward Others in the Political System*
   a. *Political Identifications*—The political units (nation, state, town, region), geographic areas, and groups to which one feels he belongs, that are in some significant subjective sense a part of his own social identity; in particular, these include those units and groups to which he feels a strong loyalty, obligation, or duty.
   b. *Political Trust*—The extent to which one feels an open, cooperative, or tolerant attitude in working with others in civic life; essentially, political trust expresses the intensity of a person's conviction that other individuals or groups mean him well (or ill) in political life.
   c. *"Rules of the Game"*—An individual's conception of what rules should be followed in civic life; these subjective preferences may or may not be consistent with prevailing law and other norms supposed to govern civic conduct.

3. *Orientations Toward One's Own Political Activity*
   a. *Political Competence*—How often, and in what manner, a person participates in civic life, the frequency with which he uses the political resources available to him in civic affairs; this may include some evaluation of his knowledge of his political resources.
   b. *Political Efficacy*—"The feeling that individual political action does have, or can have, an impact on the political process";[5] this includes a belief that political change is possible and that one can accomplish change through civic action—individuals are customarily ranked on a scale according to whether their "sense of political efficacy" is "high" or "low."

When an investigator turns his attention to the political culture of any society, he is likely to concentrate upon those political culture orientations that are *widely shared,* on the assumption that they are most likely to influence the political process because they affect the behavior of large masses. For instance, if an examination of American political culture concentrates upon political trust and reveals that a very small portion of the population exhibits a political paranoia toward Catholics, an investigator would probably consider this sentiment less important for the operation of the political system than a finding that most Americans are generally trustful, or at least tolerant, toward the political motives of other religious groups. (Of course it would be important to examine the political orientations of the anti-Catholic minority in order to understand their own political behavior.) Moreover, many of these political culture orientations are *implicit, and often unconscious, in an individual's life*—so basic that he hardly reflects upon them. In this sense, many are "primitive" orientations because they are "so implicit and taken for granted that each individual holds them and believes that all others hold them"; they become "unstated assumptions, or postulates, about politics."[6] Though held unconsciously, these beliefs and attitudes govern civic behavior, help shape the governmental order, and, for many people, define political reality. We should also note (because emphasizing a concept often seems to make it larger than life) that there is nothing metaphysical or otherwise superhuman about the operation of political culture. Political culture *expresses itself in the daily thinking and activity of people* going about the business of civic life just as their other beliefs and feelings are expressed in other aspects of the social world. Many beliefs and feelings embraced in the term "political culture" can be considered normal, commonplace, even dull—but extremely important precisely because they are so frequently commonplace; they define what is often the basic political order, the "given" in civic behavior for a society. To study political culture is, in many respects, to hold up a mirror to ourselves. We (individually and collectively) are the carriers of the culture, who not only observe it in others but also express it in our own behavior. In short, "political culture" is a conceptual shorthand for feelings, thoughts, and behaviors we note, or infer, from watching men living out their civic daily lives.

Political Culture in Operation. Ultimately, one wants to get out in societies and study their political culture by observing and interviewing people. At this point, it is clear that the components of political culture we have examined need to be "operationalized," that is, translated into a set of concrete behaviors, feelings, or opinions to study. How does one discern the direction and in-

TABLE 1.1
Some Operational Definitions of Political Culture Orientations

Orientation	Operational Definition
Political Identification	Nation of citizenship Political units and groups toward which one feels positively or negatively Political units and groups with which one is most often involved
Political Trust	Willingness to collaborate with various groups in different types of social action Group memberships Rating of groups in terms of trustworthiness, political motives, type of membership, etc.
Regime Orientations	Belief in the legitimacy of the regime Feelings toward, and evaluations of, major political offices and regime symbols Involvement in political activity supporting or opposing the regime
"Rules of the Game"	How one feels political opinions should be expressed Concepts of political obligations for oneself and others Concepts of how political decisions should be made by government Attitudes toward political deviation and dissent
Political Efficacy	Belief that government is responsive to one's opinions Belief in importance of civic activism and participation Belief in possibilities of political change
Political Competence	Frequency of voting and other types of political activity Knowledge of political events and their influence on oneself Interest in political affairs
Input-Output Orientation	Satisfaction with governmental policy Knowledge of how political demands are made on government Belief in effectiveness of policy inputs and outputs

tensity of someone's political trust? What does one ask him (or what behavior does one observe) in order to describe the "rules of the game" he supports? The problem of operationalizing the key concepts is sufficiently important to merit extended treatment later, but, for the moment, I shall suggest some common ways in which the core components have been translated into practical terms. To a great extent, this translating process depends upon the ingenuity and imagination of the investigators; one is unlikely to find two studies with identical terms.[7] Table 1.1, however, is a suggestive list. Some reflection on Table 1.1 may suggest additional ways in which the key concepts might plausibly be operationalized; the important matter, in the end, is that the concepts be reduced from abstractions to concrete terms which specify what behaviors, feelings, or attitudes one wishes to observe in the society under study.

A Growing Interest. Long before modern scholars minted the term "political culture" much of what it now includes was studied under such names as political ideology, national character, and political psychology; still, in the past several decades, political analysts have approached the topic with a greater sense of urgency and greater investments of time and resources than ever before, so that the study has reached an unprecedented intensity within the last decade. Behind this surge of interest lie several explanations. More than anything else, the pervasive political violence in the modern world, the problems of nation building in the postcolonial countries, and the recent availability of survey research methods that offer an especially useful device for enlarging our understanding of the field have stimulated a renewed interest in political culture.[8]

Political instability is now a global commonplace. Since 1945, there have been successful coups in eighteen of twenty Latin American countries, in seven Central African nations, and in six Middle Eastern and West African nations. Even the older Western European and North American nations have endured political upheavals; the boundaries and regimes of European countries have been redesigned with sometimes startling rapidity, and internal turmoil is chronic in many countries. Since World War II the Greeks, for instance, have experienced five years of civil war, several general elections involving fifty political parties, three dozen governments, three successful coups, the fall of a constitutional monarchy, three referenda, and assorted bloody political riots. In addition, the post–World War II period has spawned a host of new African and Asian nations struggling, and often failing, to create and maintain national governments in the aftermath of their colonial experience. These struggles, in particular, have forcefully raised the problems of nation building to a major concern among both scholars and statesmen involved in the quest for global peace.

These developments were especially congenial to a renewed interest in political culture, for it became apparent that explanations of political stability and nation growth, if they could be found, must go beyond an examination of different governmental forms or constitutions, or other formalities; rather, some deep probing seemed imperative to understand how emotional and attitudinal linkages are formed between members of a political community and their government and to describe how different patterns of linkage encouraged or inhibited national development and order. Moreover, such issues could not be resolved without some cross-national comparisons of political cultures; the study of political culture had to be global in its sweep. At this point, an additional incentive appeared in the development of survey research methodology, which seemed to make the empirical study of political culture especially practical by providing scholars with a technique for interviewing large numbers of individuals and obtaining detailed information about their political culture. Although the survey research technique is only one method for studying political culture (we shall shortly examine many others) it has been widely used and has undoubtedly contributed to the growing interest in the field.

The *survey research* methodology used in political culture study is an adaptation of public-opinion study techniques that have already been tested and proven in the United States and most other Western countries. Survey research enables scholars to carefully probe the civic orientations of many individuals in a multitude of national settings, to collect and process the data with great rapidity, and to apply very sophisticated techniques of interpreting the results. This means, among other things, that scholars can now go "into the field" to study national populations directly, can obtain wholly new types of information, and can tabulate results with new versatility and precision. With such new methods, not only could new questions be asked and new data collected, but there appeared the promise that for the first time a truly solid, diversified, empirical base could be provided for generalizing about patterns of political culture and their consequences.[9]

Beyond this, interest in political culture has been stimulated by the problem of bridging the gap between the "macro" and "micro" levels of political life. As survey research and other techniques provide a growing abundance of information about how individuals feel and respond to civic life, the problem arises of relating these "micro" studies of individual political behavior to the performance of whole political systems or major subunits— the "macro" level of analysis. The concept of political culture seems to offer an intellectual link between individual behavior and the survival and performance of political systems, because it relates the general to the particular. Many analysts reason that the essential components of political culture, that is, the individual orientations, must ultimately have a powerful influence upon the performance of whole political systems, so that these individual attitudes can be related to the political order in which they evolve.[10]

The bond between system performances and mass political orientations is not a fact but, rather, a working hypothesis that spurs investigators to test its validity; the incentive is that the results, should they show a strong link between political culture and political system performance, would provide an enormous "payoff" in the form of a greater understanding of the foundations of political order and chaos.

VARIATION AND CHANGE IN POLITICAL CULTURE

One essential, and intriguing, question about political culture is, How does it develop and change? This issue arises in different ways. Looking at a nation which has experienced more than a century of general political order and great continuity in its political institutions, a researcher suspects that there must be considerable stability within its political culture and seeks to discover how this is maintained. Another researcher, observing a once stable system degenerating into political violence, wonders if one explanation may be a sudden disruption in the traditional political culture and looks for the source. Yet another researcher, studying a newly developing nation, traces many of its difficulties in reaching a consensus on the form of its government to different patterns of political culture within the system; he wants to know why differing cultural patterns persist. In such ways, it becomes apparent that any understanding of political culture must, at some point, explain the origin, development, and change of the particular system under consideration. Let us examine several formative influences upon political culture generally believed to be important.

Political Socialization. To many analysts, the study of political culture begins with the maxim "political behavior is learned behavior." They assert that a person's political orientations are powerfully shaped by the individuals and institutions that influence him early in life, particularly by home, school, and friends. In general, political socialization refers to the "process whereby the individual learns his political values, attitudes, beliefs and behaviors."[11] In the perspective of political socialization, an individual is born, psychologically, the citizen of no land; he does not know what government is "his," is ignorant of the officials, symbols, rituals, and values he is supposed to honor or despise, and must be taught his political identity. In his earliest years, therefore, a person is likely to be taught the most fundamental political orientations he is expected to have—that is, he first acquires the rudiments of political culture under the powerful molding force of institutions to which he is deeply attached and from which he is especially open to influence. Of course, individuals "learn" about politics throughout their lives and, in varying degrees, alter political perspectives; virtually no one enters adulthood with an immutable political orientation. In many political systems, apparently, persons who become members of the political elite are socialized into the values, behaviors, and attitudes considered appropriate to their position at a much later time in life than they acquire their basic orientations toward the political order. Generally, it appears that the nature and extent of one's political socialization in a society may depend upon the population group to which one belongs and what political role one will play in it. Still, analysts place great emphasis upon early learning because they believe it is particularly influential and resistant to later change. In fact, one scholar asserts that the major point of early socialization is "induction into the political culture."[12]

When study moves to political socialization, attention centers upon two questions: (1) which institutions are most active in socializing individuals into a political system? and (2) what is the content of the political information communicated to individuals? As one compares political systems, it is apparent that the political socialization of the young will often be the responsibility of very different institutions, and that the nature of the material taught will vary enormously. In the United States, most Western European nations, and Great Britain, most early socialization is handled by family and school; in Communist countries, however, a child may be exposed early and continually to socialization through organizations representing the Communist Party and may, indeed, be taken out of the family for long periods of time and given intensive experience in Party-inspired work and recreation programs. In some nations, religious denominations attempt to shape the political perceptions of growing children. It is impossible to list all the religious, political, ethnic, or vocational groups that might play a part in socializing children into political life, for it is always a matter to be determined on a country-by-country basis.

In the same manner, the content of political socialization varies enormously between nations. In the United States, for example, the schools largely confine socialization to teaching "good citizenship," which usually means inculcating a respect for government and community, teaching the basic rituals of the political system (voting, for example), and instilling interest and pride in civic history. In other systems, by way of contrast, children may be taught early to have strong attachments to particular leaders, ideologies, and parties, and to have equally strong hostility to current enemies of the state or party; the spectacle of kindergarten children in the People's Republic of China playing games involving guerilla wars against "capitalist aggressors" is a graphic illustration of how far ideological war can be carried into the basic socialization scheme of a nation. Again, it is less important at this point to identify national patterns of socialization than to develop a sensitivity to the range and variety of socializing agents and the political messages they convey.

In political systems with considerable continuity of governmental institutions and stable civic processes, political socialization is most likely to be a conservative process, initiating new generations into the political values and behaviors of the ongoing system or inducing relatively modest change. Indeed, many analysts assert that the continuing stability of a political system depends, in good measure, upon the ability of the socialization process to perform this conservative function. It is understandable, then, why newly established regimes advocating changed ideologies and governmental structures are likely to place such enormous emphasis upon controlling the educational system and on managing other institutions which educate the young. New modes of socialization are used to bring coming generations under the banner of the new movement.

Despite the plausibility of these assertions about the impact of political socialization on political culture, most of them have yet to be proven. It is known that there is some carry-over of political values, attitudes, and behaviors from childhood education into adulthood—in most European nations and the United States, for example, adult party preference and attitudes toward major policy problems seem to be moderately correlated with childhood learning.[13] At the same time, there are: no conclusive evidence that most adults largely reproduce political orientations learned in childhood, no firm evidence about which institutions are likely to be most effective in childhood political learning, and few empirical studies closely following changes in political orientation through the lifetime of a sample of individuals. In many respects, this lack of information arises from the difficulty of obtaining reliable information about childhood socialization from adults and from obstacles to isolating a set of individuals for study through the life cycle. But an important additional problem is the inability of researchers to get access to populations in non-Western societies (particularly Communist systems) and the consequent poverty of data available for making generalizations on a truly cross-cultural basis. Thus, the most reasonable conclusion seems to be that far more empirical studies are needed before the role of political socialization in political culture development can be accurately assessed.

Historical Experience. Another very broad category of factors that affect individual orientations toward political systems are those events and experiences encountered through the life cycle after childhood socialization is past. Because political learning is a lifelong process and political orientations are, to some degree, susceptible to change in most people, we naturally expect an adult's political views and behaviors to respond, in some manner, to the historical events that form part of his own life.

Not all historical events, of course, are equally relevant to the study of political culture. To begin, it is often important to know which events people see as politically significant; this may not be obvious. In general, most of us select from the welter of events in our lives only certain ones to which we attribute a political meaning; it is these, consciously or unconsciously, which are likely to affect our concepts of how political life is, or should be, conducted. In traditional societies, for example, any official efforts to alter customary religious or language practices, to substitute newer life styles for old, or to otherwise "modernize" social behavior are likely to generate intense involvement, passion, and (often) opposition from many groups. These issues, far from being regarded as mere policy matters, are likely to generate strong attachments or aversions to the basic political structure. Again, in polities where any major involvement in international competition is considered a matter of national prestige, even in the case of sports or cultural events, victory and defeat may become interwoven with public judgments about the system's political performance. These examples suggest another important consideration for relating historical events to political culture: attention should be confined to those events which affect the *basic* orientations we have described. For example, a nation may endure a long period of rampant inflation. Most citizens might suffer greatly and wonder why the government is unable to control the economy; this may lead to more profound questions about the value and effectiveness of their basic governmental institutions. In this case, an investigator is likely to conclude that the inflation, with its attendant problems, has an important impact upon the political culture (specifically, "regime orientations") because citizen support for existing governmental structures is diminished. But the inflation could affect the citizens differently. Most people might conclude that a different set of economic policies, or different leaders, are needed to deal with the issue. In this instance, the investigator would probably assert that basic political culture orientations are not affected by the economic difficulties since citizen support for the governmental system seems unaffected.

The events most likely to affect a nation's political culture are those affecting great masses of people directly, profoundly, and tangibly—wars, depressions, and other crises. Such events throw the capacities of government into sharp relief, causing people to become deeply involved in political life and, often, testing and examining their basic feelings, beliefs, and assumptions about it. Major social crises often leave profound impressions upon mass political orientations. In Germany and Japan, the disastrous management of World War II, leading to the desolation of both nations, left the existing regimes and their ideologies badly discredited among large segments of the population; this situation made the task of reconstructing the governments of West Germany and Japan along more democratic lines considerably easier. Deep aversion to the prewar forms of government has remained in both nations. The United States Government's role in Vietnam, together with the administrations' failure to maintain public support for continued involvement, left large masses of Americans, especially the young, alienated from the system (at least temporarily). The civil wars in Northern Ireland, the Congo, and Algeria made establishment of national governments by consensus extremely difficult, since the violence spawned deep political distrust among major religious and social factions in those nations. It is not only dramatic events, however, which cause mass political orientations to develop and change significantly; like water on the rock, a slow but steady succession of occurrences may gradually wear away old values and replace them with new ones. It is important to recognize that political learning is lifelong and that basic political orientations often alter with the passage of time and circumstance.

Socio-economic Variables. A common discovery in political culture studies is that political orientations are often strongly associated with the socio-economic characteristics of populations. This means that variations among socio-economic groups within a polity tend to include significantly different patterns of political culture. This is one reason for the well-known fact that in virtually no society is there a political culture pattern typical of almost all individuals or social groups; group political orientations strongly deviant from the predominant one in a society are called "subcultures." Evidence of socio-economic influence on political orientations abounds. In the United States, studies reveal that trust in government and confidence in the effectiveness of political action through traditional forms is diminished among blacks, Indians, and other minorities who feel the force of discrimination; in African nations, where regional and tribal loyalties are often very strong, the political groups or governmental units to which an individual feels most strongly attached may depend upon his tribal lineage, place of residence, or family background.[14] One of the major tasks in political culture research is to identify these socio-economic variations in a society and to describe them. Almost any socio-economic characteristics may be associated with variations in political orientation within a society; the ones most frequently noted are race, occupation, family or caste, education, and income.

There are several reasons why social factors are so often associated with variations in political orientation. Frequently, political status within a society is determined by social status; since political rights, obligations, and benefits may be tied to social position, it is quite likely that individuals with different social backgrounds will have quite divergent views of political life. Social groups privileged with easy access to government, considerable material rewards from the system, and other indulgences may understandably feel more attached to the dominant institutions and values of civic life than those who are, in various ways, deprived or discriminated against. Moreover, it often happens that social status within societies is tied to education; those within the middle and upper levels of the social hierarchy, having received better education than those in lower social classes, may feel more confident of their political skills, better informed about civic life, and more aware and interested in political life, and may demonstrate many other political orientations that differ from those of less educated individuals. Finally, differing social characteristics may lead to very different expectations about what government should do: Landowners and laborers, creditors and debtors, professionals and nonprofessionals are not likely to seek the same ends from civic life nor receive the same satisfactions; social cleavages within societies are almost always rich in potential clashes of political interest and in varying assessments of how well the system operates or should operate.

Political Variables. Any list of the factors shaping and modifying political culture would be incomplete without attention to government itself and to political parties. No group has a greater stake in the development and change of political culture than does a nation's governmental elite, for their continued existence and effectiveness may depend, in the long run, upon how the mass of people are oriented toward them and toward the political institutions they manage. All governments place heavy emphasis upon controlling the major institutions of political socialization (especially the educational system) and on prescribing, in varying degrees, what shall be taught; the intent is to produce a mass political culture compatible with the regime and, once this is achieved, to preserve it.[15] In cases where a major change in regime may occur within a society—a "modernizing" elite taking the reins of government from a traditional one or a Communist regime succeeding a non-Communist one—the new government often places a high priority upon the reshaping of the political culture through the re-education of children and adults into the new allegiances and values they are expected to have with the change of political order. In these instances, no longer rare, the regime becomes the most powerful agent in remolding a political culture.[16]

In many polities, political parties play a major role in shaping mass political orientations. This may be in collaboration with, or opposition to, the dominant regime. In totalitarian countries, it is common for the single dominant party to be an organ of the regime and to penetrate all major social, occupational, cultural, and political aspects of life, taking the lead in teaching and rewarding whatever political orientations are desired by the regime. In many societies, however, political parties are part of the regime's opposition (and, in some cases, may be prohibited from overt activity); they may submit members to intensive indoctrination with political values, loyalties, and attitudes quite hostile to the dominant regime or some of the other political parties—the common situation, for instance, when Marxist parties operate in non-Marxist systems. The impact of party indoctrination will vary, of course, among political systems. In the United States, Great Britain, and most other Western European countries the dominant parties share a basic agreement on the nature of the constitutional order and the proper political processes for the nation; pronounced differences in party programs show up with respect to policy rather than regime norms. Thus, as a rule, party members are not likely to possess sharply different political culture attributes by virtue of belonging to different parties. By contrast, parties which represent regional, social, religious, or other interests sharply at variance with the dominant regime may well be socializing members into a very different cultural orientation from those found in other parties.[17]

This by no means exhausts the number of factors which may be important in shaping or transforming a political culture. Nor should one treat what has been said about the shaping of political culture as some unalterable truth. In reality, all the factors we have suggested as important in shaping political culture, and all the ways in which they seem to affect that culture, should be considered as working hypotheses—the best approximation to the truth we can make with the information now available to us. Our view of political culture is largely shaped by the methods and data at hand; as new methods of inquiry become available and new sources of information open up, our understanding of the forces shaping political culture is bound to change. In one sense, this is frustrating to both researcher and reader. It is far more satisfying to be told "the truth" about political culture than to be told what "seems" to be the truth. In another sense, however, the tentativeness of our conclusions leaves us open to new information and new arguments. This keeps the imagination flexible and guards against dogmatism. Moreover, it underscores how dependent we are on our techniques of study for the conclusions we reach. Indeed, it is not possible to judge the adequacy of our understanding of political culture unless we know how the information is gathered and what strengths or weaknesses lie in our methods. Thus, it is both logical and necessary to examine, briefly, how our conclusions about political culture are formed. This means turning to the techniques for the study of political culture.

TOOLS OF EVIDENCE AND INFERENCE

As the study of political culture has broadened and intensified, the variety of techniques utilized by investigators has increased in sophistication and number so that an enormous range of procedures currently exists. Let us examine the most common of them.

Cross-national Comparisons. Political culture study today usually involves the collection and comparison of data from a multitude of differing cultures; the objective is to develop a fund of information about a wide range of cultures from which to draw generalizations of greater breadth and insight than would be accessible if one concentrated upon a single political culture. Single-culture studies are done, of course; they are the building blocks of the larger comparisons. However, investigators feel that cross-national comparisons are more powerful investigative tools and ought to be the ultimate goal of political culture research.

The basic reason for this cross-cultural preoccupation is the attempt to avoid "culture-bound" conclusions about political life. This problem exists because most researchers have been raised in Western cultures and might, however unwittingly, assume that the "facts" of political culture (or the proper interpretations of the facts) are those familiar in Western societies. A study of less familiar, non-Western societies almost always reveals some of these culture-bound notions. For example, scholars discovered that some traditional and primitive societies include many individuals who have no concept of "government" nor any word for the concept in their vocabularies.[18] There are other compelling reasons for seeking cross-cultural comparisons. Having available data on many cultures can greatly expand the range of variation of some factor whose influence upon political attitudes the investigator wants to study; thus, to observe how the creation of a state church affects political loyalties, the researcher can compare societies having such an institution to those without one. Moreover, many traditional societies and other unique social settings are fast disappearing, vanishing in the wake of "modernization" as relentlessly as rare animals and habitats under the pressure of civilization. It may soon be difficult, or impossible, to study the political culture of purely agrarian societies or of nations unaffected by the political manipulation of large powers.[19] Then, too, one is better able to evaluate his own political culture when he has knowledge of other cultures to provide perspective and insight.

Useful as they are, cross-national studies pose formidable, but not necessarily insurmountable, problems for the investigator; many of these problems relate to the use of the survey research method.

Survey Research. The basic tool of contemporary political culture study is the survey research method.[20] Survey research, a refinement of the techniques used in public-opinion polling, is commonly used for gathering cross-national data on mass orientations toward civic life. Typically, a survey research study will involve at least the following steps:

1. creation of a *research design* in which the purpose of study, the nations to be included, the general content of the survey, and other objectives are specified
2. development of a *survey questionnaire* to be administered to selected population groups in the countries to be studied
3. organization and training of the *research team*, including interviewers, supervisors, data coders, and interpreters
4. *pretesting* of the questionnaire and rehearsing of procedures for the organizational units

5. drawing of the *sample* to be interviewed in the communities selected for study
6. going into the *field* to obtain the interviews
7. collection, coding, computer run, and interpretation of *data*

Most researchers would be delighted, and surprised, if their operations went this smoothly. Cross-national surveys are customarily expensive undertakings—an ambitious one can easily approach half a million dollars to underwrite—and securing sponsorship itself is often an arduous task. Whenever data must be obtained from other nations (particularly non-Western ones) the organizational problems alone prove substantial, and other obstacles must be anticipated: the questionnaire must be worded, tested, and administered in a manner appropriate to the nation being studied; the interviewers must be constantly checked and supervised; and the data must be properly interpreted. The availability of computers to interpret interview material, manipulate it statistically, and arrange it in almost any manner dictated by the researcher has made possible the rapid gathering and organization of data. Computers also enable researchers to "ask" their data questions which could not be put previously because the data themselves, and rapid means to process them, were lacking.

Of all the tasks which challenge the researcher's patience and ingenuity, none exceed the job of sampling and interviewing. Good sampling is an absolute requirement for a useful cultural study. The purpose of sampling is to select a small portion of a population (the "sample") which, when observed, will yield reliable information about the larger population (the "universe"). Although the size of a sample may not be particularly large— samples used to represent whole nations seldom exceed 2,000 individuals—and although statistically sound methods are readily available for this task, the job can turn into an ordeal, particularly when developing nations are the subject. Sometimes, reliable census data or other aggregate information used as a basis for sampling is incomplete or unavailable; populations may be so mobile that most individuals have disappeared before they can be interviewed. A common problem in the impoverished areas of many underdeveloped nations is that "blocks" with neatly arranged residential units, such as those in most Western countries, may not exist; often the interviewers—who are frequently instructed to sample on the basis of housing units and streets—arrive in the field only to find an enormous sprawl of hovels, shanties, or other structures, and no "streets" at all. Sometimes imagination comes to the rescue; sometimes a whole new procedure has to be invented to get a sample. (One team, discovering common walkways through a squatters' village, used these as streets for sampling purposes; another team found that when they marked houses with a chalk "X" to indicate places where interviews should take place, the owner frequently erased the mark, fearing an "evil eye" had been put on his house.)[21]

Assuming a sample can be drawn, the interviewing can be difficult. Many governments are quite suspicious of foreign-sponsored research within their borders; the issues and questions with which the interviews deal often involve delicate or sensitive subjects, which respondents may be hesitant to discuss. (One can wonder how Americans might react to a study of political opinions in the United States sponsored by Soviet researchers.) Sometimes native interviewers (usually the most desirable) treat the study as a game; they may, occasionally, fabricate interviews or "contaminate" the interviews that do occur by bias of many kinds. Quite often, cross-cultural studies prosper or decline according to the temperature of diplomatic relations between the host country and the one sponsoring the research.

Despite such obstacles, cross-cultural survey research has been the most common foundation for political culture study in recent years. Of course, there are many instances in which other techniques are used as substitutes or supplements; sometimes, alternatives are unavoidable.

Content Analysis. Some political systems are virtually sealed against the survey researcher, particularly those in the Soviet bloc, so that indirect methods must be used to infer as much as possible about the character of the political culture. One such indirect technique is *content analysis* which involves a systematic monitoring of the content found in the media, speeches of public officials, public documents, and the host of other materials produced in the course of civic life. Hazards abound in this procedure and scholars continue to disagree over its merit, but it can prove, under proper circumstances, a useful adjunct for studying political culture.

Essentially, content analysis has been defined as "information-processing in which communication content is transformed, through objective and systematic application of categorization and rules, into data that can be summarized and compared."[22] This technique, developed in the 1940's, has been used for diverse purposes; among others, to analyze the content of military intelligence, to reveal the psychology of individuals by examining their communications, and to verify the authorship of documents. A variety of disciplines have come to employ this method, and political science produces roughly one-fifth of all content studies. The procedure customarily begins with a research question the investigator poses to his data. In a recent study, for instance, an investigator wanted to know what political norms the Castro regime was attempting to nurture among very young Cubans.[23] Once the question is formed, the media to be studied are selected—in our example, Communist Party youth manuals used in the Cuban grammar schools. Then the investigator specifies the set of ideas, objects, persons, or other data he wants to study and structures these as categories of information to be compiled; in the Cuban study, categories included words and phrases dealing with loyalty to the government, animosity toward the United States, dedication to greater economic productivity, and so forth. Then, having obtained the raw communications, the researcher trains coders to read or otherwise monitor the material, noting and counting the frequency with which key items appear in the media. Finally, the investigator interprets his data in line with his purposes and the limits of the available material. This, of course, is a severe simplification of the content analysis method, but it suggests the logic underlying the system.

Content analysis has been applied to many aspects of political culture. Studies of official speeches and documents often yield an insight into the norms a regime is most anxious to establish or feels are particularly endangered; mass-circulation magazines may be sifted to discover the extent to which the content is a device for propagandizing readers or otherwise communicating political ideas. Sometimes, public letters sent to official or quasi-official newspapers and magazines are scanned to estimate the nature and extent of "deviant" political behavior in a society. In a recent study of the Soviet Union, letters to several labor publications and cultural digests were carefully evaluated to determine what facets of the Soviet economy the citizens found either most satisfactory or least acceptable.[24] As with most other research tools, the uses of content analysis depend to a great degree upon the imagination of the researcher. Content analysis has not yet proven to be a satisfactory research tool for primary information gathering about political culture but, rather, a useful adjunct to other methods.

Elite Studies. Political analysts almost universally assume that political systems are stratified in terms of political power and that a relatively small proportion of the populations exercise most of this power. These *elite* are commonly the focus of intensive study in political culture research. Given a reliable procedure for identifying a nation's political elite—and all methods are open to controversy—the description of the elite's orientations and a comparison of them with mass political culture is almost essential in any competently comprehensive profile of a nation's political culture. Elites are often quite visible; they are customarily articulate, informed, and reflective about political life and their role in it (which means, capable of offering the insights into their political behavior so often lacking in mass interviews). Even when elites are not directly accessible, their orientations may be widely advertised and reported. But far more than visibility and convenience prompts such close scrutiny.

Political elites are studied, essentially, because their political values, attitudes, and behaviors are most likely to set the dominant political style and tone of a nation's civic life, to determine the system's response to internal and external stress, to define the critical political values of a nation, and to shape the future political orientations and experiences of the masses. In brief, elites often manage the system and fashion it in their image. Then, too, they may epitomize with particular clarity the dominant political orientations of the population as a whole, thereby offering an investigator a keen insight into the operant political orientations of the broader culture. When no such congruence exists between elite and mass political culture, the nature of the differences and the potential tensions between the two cultures becomes an important dimension of cultural analysis. At the outset of research, the degree of comparability between elite and mass political culture should always be regarded as a question to be investigated. Most often, however, investigators believe that, in stable political orders, the elite are the "carriers of the culture," in the sense that they are the most significant actors in shaping the nature of national civic life.

Apart from the usual problems encountered when attempting to determine the political orientations of any set of individuals, elite studies are complicated by the need to devise a reliable method for identifying the members of the elite. This is often no simple task, for the true wielders of power may camouflage their existence behind formal leaders who have only fictional authority. There may be no single, well-defined leadership cadre in a society on most issues, and expeditions in search of leaders may find only hostility, confusion, and frustration. Moreover, scholars have generated volumes of material in their continuing debate over the proper technique for identifying the true political elite in a society. For all these reasons, the task of properly identifying and describing the political culture of civic elites requires a major investment of time, ingenuity, and money.

National-Character Studies. Political scientists have occasionally assumed the existence of *national character* as a device for describing aspects of political culture—a procedure sure to generate argument. This concept, borrowed from anthropology and social psychology (the disciplines which first experimented with it), assumes that the patterned conditions of life within a society create certain distinctive personality types, or *social characters.* Presumably, a researcher can identify these distinctive personality types and use them to interpret how individuals respond to their social milieu, including their political system.[25] Perhaps the simplest definition of *national character* is that it includes personality types that are common or standardized within a social system; these are often called *modal* types. There may be several modal types in a society and, in complex societies, a great many.

In the study of political culture, the assumption of a national character implies that certain types of political orientation are so common to a nation that citizens are very likely to fall into one of them. Thus, national character refers not primarily to how people behave but to underlying personality structures that are essentially alike for large numbers of individuals (running, presumably, into the millions in large societies) and that determine responses to civic life. For example, one common explanation of the rise of fascism in Germany during the 1930's was the existence of an "authoritarian personality" among the German masses; this national-character type was also used, in another variation, to explain the rise of totalitarian political systems in other countries, and, even more generally, to describe the type of person anywhere who was favorably disposed to authoritarian systems.

Modern studies of national character are often conducted with careful regard for the concept's limitations and with responsible use of evidence, yet considerable skepticism about their worth remains. Quite often, the empirical data supporting various descriptions of "modal personalities" appear flimsy and superficial; frequently, assertions about the existence of national character are made after observing collective behavior, rather than by the more convincing method of carefully examining the psychological makeup of individuals within a society. Moreover, national-character studies (particularly very early ones) were sometimes used in a clumsy attempt to rationalize various racist dogmas; even responsible scholars were occasionally guilty of salting their material with liberal doses of their own prejudices, often unwittingly. Understandably, this potential for abuse has left scholars a bit wary of the national-character concept. In recent years, however, some political scientists have joined the concept of modal personality to survey research data about large samples of national populations, thus producing a more appealing synthesis. Essentially, the technique is to discover, if possible, certain recurrent patterns of feeling, attitude, and belief among sample populations and to identify these as typical orientations to civic life— a description which does not imply the existence of whole personality types likely to respond in typical ways to all aspects of social life. The burden of proof, in effect, is considerably less than in arguments made for traditional national characters. Still, national-character studies of any kind are not a major form of political culture study and are not likely to be for some time; the verdict of most scholars remains, in the words of one writer, that national-character analysis continues to be "an important but problematic" concept.[26]

History as a Political Laboratory. All of history can be said to constitute an immense repository of potentially valuable information about political culture. Indeed, history is the only "laboratory" in which assumptions about the effect of political culture on civic life are tested and the only place we can go to learn about factors shaping political culture itself. The narrative of historical events tells us the manifold ways in which political culture has operated, and continues to operate, on civic life. It is essential, of course, to be sensitive to the many specialized tools available for studying political culture. In many ways, however, the most valuable and creative tool remains the inquiring mind that probes through history in search of clues (past or present) to political culture's operation. It is true that reliance upon historical documents often means depending upon information gathered and interpreted by others; there can seldom be a trip into the field to expand data, refine techniques, or pursue interesting leads. Reliance upon historical data, in this perspective, often seems less satisfying (or accurate) than using newer techniques applied to purely contemporary civic cultures. Still, we are wholly dependent upon historical narratives and documents for any conclusions, or even guesses, we might make about political culture preceding the past few decades; it is the historical chronicle that tells us almost all we know about political culture through most of man's stay on the planet. Thus, to narrow our interest in political culture to the brief time frame of contemporary events, and to rest our insight entirely upon what such modern survey research can reveal, is to take a very crabbed and unimaginative approach to the subject.

SOME PROBLEMS IN POLITICAL CULTURE RESEARCH

It is well to conclude by briefly mentioning several characteristic problems encountered in any cross-national study of civic life.

All cross-national studies (and even some conducted between divergent culture groupings within the same nation) are open to
challenges relating to the degree of *equivalence* in the study and
to the *validity* and *reliability* of the data. These problems are not
insurmountable but an investigator must be prepared to demonstrate that he has plausibly solved the issues posed. Anyone wish-
ing to evaluate the quality of a cross-national study must understand the importance of *equivalence* and of data *reliability* and
validity as standards of judgment.

The Equivalence Problem. This is perhaps the most nettlesome
and certainly the most unavoidable of all conceptual difficulties
in cross-national research. Ideally, a researcher seeks *equivalence*
in the data and concepts he is comparing between cultures; he
wants assurance, when comparing similar ideas, attitudes, or behaviors across cultures, that he has actually obtained equivalent
information. Conclusions drawn from cross-national comparisons
almost always assume the equivalence of much information; data
equivalence is so absolute a requirement that a failure to approach this goal usually renders both data and conclusions very
suspect.[27] As a practical matter, it is often impossible to prove
that data or concepts are absolutely equivalent, but their degree
of similarity can usually be estimated.

The problem arises because political concepts, attitudes, and
behaviors—even the words of the political vocabulary—which
have a fixed meaning in one culture may be quite differently interpreted in another, or may mean little. Thus, concepts, interview questions, and data interpretations based upon assumptions
that particular words, attitudes, or activities have essentially the
same meaning across several cultures can be grossly mistaken.
The tendency of political words, attitudes, and behaviors to take
on distinctive colorations in different cultures is often attributed
to *system interference,* and the task of the researcher is to mini-
mize the effect of this interference on his data or to fully recognize its existence and take account of it when evaluating his findings. In either case, a competent investigator will usually take
precautions to be sure that system interference is considered
when presenting his findings.

Equivalence problems usually arise at several specific points in a cross-national study, beginning with the operationalization of important concepts in different cultures. An investigator wants comparable measures of "political participation" between an industrialized Western nation and a traditional society; he may decide that voting is a useful indicator in the West but questions whether this is true in a traditional society. Might not an individual's political involvement in a traditional society be more appropriately measured by his activity in tribal, religious, or other community groups, where many important political decisions may be made? Indeed, it is possible that the society may place no positive value upon political participation at all; the investigator could not necessarily conclude that low participation meant alienation from the civic culture. The equivalence problem may also arise in the wording of questions. Suppose an investigator wishes to know how people in several cultures react to public officials and decides to use the word "politician" in a study in the United States. He must be very careful to use a word equivalent to this (if he can find one) when interviewing members of other cultures; sometimes, no such word exists or the literal counterpart has quite different connotations. Finally, it is necessary to look for equivalence even in the atmosphere of the interview itself. For instance, in some cultures (but not others) there is a traditional "courtesy set" encountered when talking with respondents; they will attempt to answer questions in the manner they think is most satisfactory (or least offensive) to the interviewer. Such examples are almost endless but they underscore the criticalness of the equivalence issue.

The Problem of Validity. The issue of validity (like the matter of *reliability* discussed next) is not unique to cross-national studies but arises in any effort to measure opinions, attitudes, and behaviors. The measurement of a feeling, attitude, or behavior—whether a question, a set of questions, or some other indicator—is said to be *valid* "when it measures what it purports to measure."[28] A valid measure of political cynicism estimates a person's degree of political cynicism and not his degree of political activism; an estimate of one's political information is valid when it probes this and not one's political interest. For the investigator, the question is, Am I measuring what I think I am measuring?

The answer to this question is often difficult to provide in the case of survey research questionnaires unless they are exhaustively tested and analyzed through a variety of sophisticated, time-consuming, and expensive procedures. The problem, however, can be easily demonstrated. A scholar wants to know whether a set of respondents are politically cynical and, if so, to what degree. He decides that a good measure would be the extent to which the respondents believe major governmental officials are usually honest. He may first decide to ask his respondents whether they believe the current President (or Prime Minister or other national leader) "wants to do what is best for the people." Upon reflection, he may decide that such a question measures how the respondent feels about the particular person then holding office, whereas he would rather know how the respondent feels, more generally, about most public officials. So, he may ask his respondent to react to a statement such as "I think most public officials want to do what is best most of the time." In short, the investigator assumes that the latter procedure will produce a more valid measure of attitude than the earlier formula.

This example somewhat oversimplifies the task of determining the validity of questions but does suggest how the problem arises and why it must be resolved. In any event, it is one of the necessary jobs in questionnaire construction for cross-national survey research.

The Reliability Problem. A technique for measuring a political attitude, feeling, or behavior is considered *reliable* when it yields similar results under similar conditions. "If we measure the same set of objects again and again with the same or comparable measuring instruments, will we get the same or similar results?" At first glance, this may not seem a difficult problem. All that is required, apparently, is that when the same technique is used in the same situation on the same individual or individuals, it should yield approximately the same results. However, this apparently uncomplicated, straightforward issue can easily confound a survey study unless it is carefully noted, and its implications investigated, when the survey is designed.

Let us illustrate the reliability problem. Suppose a researcher desired interviews with 1,500 Chileans and, among other matters, sought to estimate their political activism. He has devised a measure of political activism including the following question: "How often have you voted in elections during the last five years?" He is likely to discover that when his question was administered there was confusion concerning *which* elections were involved. Were local, district, or national elections to be included and were other types of contests (union elections, for instance) involved? It is likely that different respondents interpreted this question divergently and that many did not interpret it as the author intended; moreover, those workers who actually did the field interviews (large surveys are customarily farmed out to a host of hired interviewers) may have given contradictory answers to different individuals when asked to clarify the question. In this case, two interviewers might have spoken to the same person and, using the same question, arrived at two differing estimates of political activism. The instrument (question) was clearly unreliable.

Careful examination of question wording and interpretation is one way to maximize reliability in surveys. Another test of reliability involves the correspondence between a respondent's report of his behavior and other information which can verify the report. (If a question deals with political activism, it may be possible to obtain data on the respondent's past voting through registration lists, polling lists, or other data.) Particularly, in the case of political culture studies, the investigator would like the reliability of his study to extend to predictions about future behavior (although this is difficult to achieve). This could mean that he wants reliable self-estimates of how an individual or group is likely to behave but, equally important, he might want to tap the variety of psychological attitudes and beliefs that are of such fundamental importance to individuals that they will orient future behavior, whether or not this is consciously recognized by the individuals involved.

Although other problems commonly arise in cultural studies, those we have described are customarily the most serious and demand, in any case, the expenditure of time, money, and manpower to expunge from cultural investigations. With some idea of the logic and techniques involved in political culture study, we can now turn, in the next chapter, to how political culture has been described.

NOTES

1. This definition suggested by Lucian W. Pye and Sidney Verba, *Political Culture and Political Development* (Princeton: Princeton University Press, 1965), p. 7. For other definitions, see Donald J. Devine, *The Political Culture of the United States* (Boston: Little, Brown, 1972), chapter 1; and Gabriel Almond and G. Bingham Powell, Jr., *Comparative Politics: A Developmental Approach* (Boston: Little, Brown, 1966), chapter 3.

2. Sidney Verba, "Comparative Political Culture," in Pye and Verba, *op. cit.*, p. 518.

3. This definitional thicket is described in Yong C. Kim, "The Concept of Political Culture," *Journal of Politics*, 26 (May, 1964), 313–36.

4. Lucian W. Pye, *Aspects of Political Development* (Boston: Little, Brown, 1966), pp. 104–5.

5. Angus Campbell, Gerald Gurin, and Warren E. Miller, *The Voter Decides* (Evanston, Ill.: Row, Peterson, 1954), p. 187.

6. Verba, *op. cit.*, p. 519.

7. Different operational definitions can be compared in Gabriel Almond and Sidney Verba, *The Civic Culture* (Princeton: Princeton University Press, 1963); Devine, *op. cit.;* and the numerous articles in Pye and Verba, *op. cit.*

8. The importance of survey research technology to political culture research is well illustrated in Frederick W. Frey, "Cross-Cultural Research in Political Science," in Robert T. Holt and John E. Turner (eds.), *The Methodology of Comparative Research* (New York: The Free Press, 1970), pp. 173–295.

9. The most productive cross-national materials so far produced deal with comparative socialization patterns. See, for example, Robert D. Hess, "The Socialization of Attitudes Toward Political Authority: Some Cross-National Comparisons"; and Jack Dennis, Leon Lindberg, Donald McCrone, and Rodney Stiefbold, "Political Socialization to Democratic Orientations in Four Western Systems," in Lewis Bowman and G. R. Boynton (eds.), *Political Behavior and Public Opinion* (Englewood Cliffs, N.J.: Prentice-Hall, 1974).

10. See Almond and Verba, *op. cit.*, chapter 1, for this discussion.

11. A useful summary of political socialization studies is found in Dean Jaros, *Socialization to Politics* (New York: Praeger Publishers, 1973); and in Thomas J. Cook and Frank P. Scioli, Jr., "Political Socialization Research in the United States: A Review," in Dan D. Nimmo and Charles M. Bonjean (eds.), *Political Attitudes and Public Opinion* (New York: David McKay, 1972), pp. 154–74.

12. Cook and Scioli, *op. cit.*

13. See, for instance, Philip E. Converse and Georges Dupeux, "Politicization of the Electorate in France and the United States," *Public Opinion Quarterly*, 26 (Spring, 1962), 1–23; and Angus Campbell and Henry Valen, "Party Identification in Norway and the United States," *Public Opinion Quarterly*, 25 (Winter, 1961), 505–25.

14. A useful summary of the literature dealing with socio-economic factors in political culture formation is found in Richard E. Dawson and Kenneth Prewitt, *Political Socialization* (Boston: Little, Brown, 1968), chapters 7, 10.

15. The role of education in socializing individuals into political roles is nicely summarized in James S. Coleman, "Introduction: Education and Political Development," in James S. Coleman (ed.), *Education and Political Development* (Princeton, N.J.: Princeton University Press, 1965), pp. 3–34.

16. See Coleman (ed.), *op. cit.*, Part II for numerous case studies in regime-directed education.

17. On American parties, see Herbert McClosky, Paul J. Hoffman, and Rosemary O'Hara, "Issue Conflict and Consensus Among Party Leaders and Followers," *American Political Science Review*, 54 (June, 1960), 406–27.

18. For other illustrations, see Frey, *op. cit.*

19. *Ibid.*

20. The basics of survey research are summarized in Charles H. Backstrom and Gerald D. Hursh, *Survey Research* (Evanston, Ill.: Northwestern University Press, 1963).

21. Frey, *op. cit.*

22. Ole R. Holsti, *Content Analysis for the Social Sciences* (Reading, Mass.: Addison-Wesley, 1969), p. 3.

23. *Ibid.*, p. 5.

24. Ellen Mickiewicz, "Political Applications of Public Opinion Research in the Soviet Union," *Public Opinion Quarterly*, 36 (Winter, 1972–73), 566–78.

25. Alex Inkeles and Daniel J. Levinson, "National Character: The Study of Modal Personality and Sociocultural Systems," in Gardner Lindzey and Elliot Aronson (eds.), *The Handbook of Social Psychology*, vol. 4, *Group Psychology and Phenomena of Interaction* (Reading, Mass.: Addison-Wesley, 1969), pp. 418–507.

26. *Ibid.*, p. 418.

27. See Frey, *op. cit.*, or Adam Przeworki and Henry Teune, *The Logic of Comparative Social Inquiry* (New York: John Wiley and Sons, 1970), for an extended discussion of the equivalency issue.

28. Abraham Kaplan, *The Conduct of Inquiry* (San Francisco: Chandler, 1964), pp. 198 ff.

2

PATTERNS OF POLITICAL CULTURE

In one respect, a map of the world is a bit of unintended deception. It partitions the globe into different geographic areas, gives each a distinctive national boundary, a capital, and a distinguishing hue. Then this global patchwork is presented to us as a set of "nations," implying that the people within these different territories share the attributes of genuine nationhood. This is a fiction.

It is common to say that any group of people are a "nation" if they live together within the boundaries of a state outlined on the world map. To the political analyst, however, a *nation* is considerably more. It is, essentially, a group of people living within a geographic area and united by many common political values, attitudes, and loyalties; it is a political community held together by a consensus on the basic procedures governing political life —and especially, by allegiance to a common national government. In this sense, many of the world's countries are not yet nations. Indeed, much of the world's political violence can be traced to the failure of people living within states to create true national communities resting upon a broad political consensus. Instead, many nations consist of a government that asserts wavering authority over large masses of alienated subjects. Or the nation may have several rival governments, each with its own army and capital, each claiming to be legitimate. Many nations are chronically convulsed by civil war, which arises whenever major groups fail to agree upon the proper national government or have different ideas about who belongs within the nation. Some nations are constantly on the verge of disintegration into warring geographic areas that insist on independence. One of the most enduring contrasts in the world lies between those people enjoying relative peace and order arising from a true national community and those constantly exposed to the turmoil of unstable political orders.

Although many schemes have been suggested for classifying different types of political cultures, a recurrent approach has been to differentiate cultures found in stable national communities from those found in unstable ones. Out of this preoccupation with political order has gradually emerged an implicit consensus among many scholars that political cultures ought to be roughly ordered along a continuum from "fragmented" to "integrated" with many intermediate types. In formal terms, these concepts are models (or "ideal types") of political culture; no culture we observe will correspond to the prescriptions of the model in all respects. Still, this approach has been serviceable. It provides culture analysts with a working vocabulary, some useful assumptions about political culture, and a flexible set of concepts. In many respects, these concepts still remain unfinished and inelegant, a topic for continuing scholarly debate. In any case, they are firmly rooted in the logic of comparative analysis.[1]

Fragmented Political Cultures

In simple terms, a fragmented political culture is one whose population lacks broad agreement upon the way in which political life should be conducted. At the political culture level, the population separates (that is, "fragments") into groups isolated from one another by contradictory and incompatible orientations toward political life. This may involve different sets of political identifications, irreconcilable differences about what rules of the game should prevail in civic life, different regime orientations, or other conflicts. Quite often, extreme distrust exists between opposing groups. We shall shortly define the elements of a fragmented culture more carefully; for the moment, it is sufficient to note that a fragmented culture increases the feeling of isolation and disagreement among social groups, erodes consensus on political fundamentals, and inhibits the development of conditions necessary for a true national community.

Political analysts are especially interested in fragmented political cultures because many of the world's peoples are desperately attempting to overcome this fragmentation to create new nations. Many of the typical political problems found among the world's currently *developing* countries seems to arise from cultural fragmentation; the future of these states will rest, among other things, on their ability to deal successfully with this problem. Before discussing fragmentation in detail, it will be helpful to examine how this problem is related to nation building and what contributes to the growth of fragmented cultures.

Fragmentation and Nation Building. Today, the majority of fragmented political cultures are found in countries growing from rebellions against colonial regimes after World War II, although such fragmentation is also found among other nations, such as Northern Ireland, Canada, and many Latin American states. In the recent struggle to lift the colonial yoke from millions of people previously ruled by European powers, there was a common pattern. A native political elite in the colonized nation, seizing the opportunities provided by the weakening of many colonial powers and the growing demand among colonial masses for self-determination, successfully rallied the native masses and, peacefully or violently, made the continuation of colonial rule untenable; sometimes the liberation movements were abetted by the colonial nations who, no longer able to govern their historic overseas empires, were anxious (or at least willing) to grant local autonomy.[2]

The liberation of colonial empires, however, left the resulting peoples in political disarray. A new, native elite gained national power and attempted to fashion new national governments, which would function as did those in the older nation-states. What was needed was clear enough. There had to be national territory under control of a central government with established, operative authority over all subordinate political units within its ambit. The government had to be organized along the lines thought necessary in modern states; there had to be the proper institutions (executive, legislative, and administrative authorities), a means of recruiting the leadership and manpower for the national government, and the necessary authority for the government to operate. Moreover, the new governments had to do more than maintain civic order. They had to "penetrate" the society, that is, to have the governmental apparatus to reach all important social and economic sectors with authority and administrative resources; and, they had to demonstrate some "extractive" capacity, or an ability to mobilize important human and material resources to meet the nation's most urgent social problems.

Unfortunately for the nation-building elites, they customarily inherited populations ill-prepared for nationhood. The colonial territories often embraced extremely divergent populations, divided along a multitude of social, racial, and religious lines, that were held within a single political community by the military and administrative power of the colonial regime. Whatever mass political identifications developed were, characteristically, toward the colonial regime and administration rather than toward an indigenous nation. In a similar vein, the official language, political practices, and dominant cultural norms were often imported from the colonial power and, while native culture and political structures sometimes remained, they failed to achieve widespread currency and acceptance among many major social groups. In short, the colonial regimes did not emphasize the creation of a national consciousness or a sense of political community and seldom fostered the civic processes which would permit the masses to determine their own political means and ends. Suddenly, with nationhood, the elites and masses of the new nations had to develop a whole, new political psychology and a political culture capable of supporting an independent national government and political system. For the masses, particularly, this transition was abrupt and often traumatic. "The transfer of sovereignty from a colonial regime to an independent one is more than a mere shift of power from foreign hands to native ones; it is a transformation of the whole pattern of political life. . . ."[3] With the conclusion of the liberation struggle, masses and elites often found their common political objective, forged from the presence of a common enemy, had dissolved; opposition and discord evolved between elites and masses, and between rival political factions, in the new "nations." The practical problems of designing a government and of setting national priorities, of deciding who would participate in civic life and how, revealed with stark clarity that social and political fragmentation was one inheritance of the anti-colonial movement.

It is understandable, then, that one scholar familiar with the newer nations could write: "The great problem today in nation building is that of relating the administrative and authoritative structures of government to political forces within the transitional societies."[4] In short, the new governing elites had to *create*, out of the normally fragmented cultures they inherited, a political culture compatible with national development. What made this task most difficult was the inherent social pluralism of these societies, a matter which deserves attention not only for the light it sheds upon the origin of fragmented cultures, but because social pluralism, wherever they are encountered, almost always underlies the creation and perpetuation of fragmented political cultures.

Social Pluralism. Most fragmented political cultures, and certainly those of developing nations in Africa and Asia, are characterized by an enormous diversity of social groups; the social cleavages which are most often productive of political disorder, and which frustrate nation building, are those involving ethnicity and language, race, religion, caste, and regionalism.

This social pluralism need not frustrate stable national government, particularly when there is clearly a majority group sharing a broad range of compatible cultural characteristics (as happened when the United States was created), but that is not the common pattern in the developing nations. According to one estimate, fully half of the African states, forty per cent of Middle Eastern nations, and about one-third of the Asian states have no majority culture and, in many instances, do not have even a dominant culture. Occasionally (as in South Africa where the dominant white minority rules with only twenty-one per cent of the population) minorities control the political process and dictate the dominant political culture forms, but such rule is usually precarious, fraught with latent, or open, opposition from the subjugated majorities.[5] Typically, then, the new states began the arduous task of nation building with a cultural pluralism unleavened by the experience of successful national development and, quite often, without a dominant culture to ease the transition. Given such circumstances, many basic political decisions in the developing nations tended to arouse intense discord and suspicion between social groups. For instance, the process of recruiting political leaders, electing officials, and staffing the administrative apparatus of the new governments often resulted in a control of political power by religious or ethnic groups whose dominance was extremely threatening to minorities. The historic cleavage between India's Hindu majority and its Muslim minority erupted into a vicious civil war following India's independence and the control of the new state by the Hindus. The 1947 war, leaving 500,000 dead and 12 million refugees, was settled only with the creation of the new state of Pakistan for the Muslim minority—an early example of the secessionist movements common to many newer states. Even this partition did not resolve the cultural discord between Hindu and Muslim, which broke out anew in the short but bloody conflict over East Pakistan in 1972, a war which culminated in the creation of the new state of Bangladesh with India's assistance. Indeed, India's own 400 million people are a classic example of the cultural pluralism and political fragmentation of the newer nations. One study in the mid-1960s found that only 8 per cent of the people in both north and south India had "nationally oriented loyalties"; the officially designated language, Hindi, is spoken by only 40 per cent of a population that has at least eleven major linguistic groups, many quite unintelligible to each other.[6] It is not surprising, therefore, that almost all questions of official language policy —such as the language to be used in schools—are a constant source of culture conflict.

Language is only one of many divisive issues. Controversy may arise over the location of regional and local governmental centers, over which social groups will be recruited into the civil service, and over the levels and standards of such recruitments. Resource allocations—the sites for new industries, port developments, new railways, or highways—will often become (or seem) a contest with ethnic, religious, racial, and linguistic triumphs or defeats. Quite often, one result of pluralism is the emergence of political movements, frequently expressed as political parties, committed to protecting and advancing the interests of their social base against those of other groupings. In many cases, these movements fail to gain sufficient national following to become factors in national politics, or they are gradually absorbed into movements with a broader base, under the skillful leadership of an elite committed to building parties with national, rather than parochial, programs. Sometimes these movements are banned and suppressed, at other times they may lead to secessionist states in which they hold power (there are numerous patterns of development). Of course, the divisive issues in fragmented political cultures are often similar to controversial questions in more integrated societies; the issues are dangerously divisive in the newer nations because they occur in cultures where belief in governmental legitimacy, political trust, political identifications, and other political sentiments are not widely shared and, consequently, underlying civic trust and consensus on civic procedures are not available to buffer the conflict.

There are numerous ways in which the political problems created by cultural pluralism can be eased and national development continued. With time, new generations might be socialized into civic values more compatible with nationhood so that the fragmentation of the political culture could be diminished through education. Sometimes, a resolution is forced when geographically concentrated groups secede from the original state, although this is often a bloody, prolonged struggle. Many of the current states of Asia and Africa are themselves secessionist fragments from other states. Thus, Rwanda and Burundi are two parts of an original Ruanda-Urundi state, both Zambia and Malawi seceded from the Federation of Rhodesia and Nyasaland, Singapore left Malaysia, and Syria opted out of the United Arab Republic. In other instances, the stresses of cultural pluralism might be eased by the creation of a federal system which grants considerable independence for the political organization of important regional or ethnic groupings within a society, although this solution is difficult to achieve in practice; a government may also adopt a deliberate policy of cultural neutrality. Political leaders and parties may arise that have a capacity to assimilate the competing demands of many social groups into a new program that provides a viable formula for continued national development. Finally, there may be a policy of deliberate cultural suppression or extermination directed against dissident elements within the polity.

Such a brief discussion can only suggest why social pluralism and fragmented political cultures are so often associated in the newer states, but it provides some explanation of why fragmented cultures develop and persist. Against this background, we can now describe in greater detail what are likely to be the most important manifestations of fragmentation within a political culture.

Facets of Fragmentation. If it were possible to take an inventory of mass political orientations within a fragmented political culture, one would expect to find most, or all, of the following conditions:

1. *A dominance of parochial political loyalties over national ones.* It is common to find in fragmented political cultures that a large proportion of the population is bonded by intense emotional ties of loyalty and identification to those groups and institutions which represent local, regional, or other subnational interests. These *parochial* ties may be formed to tribe or family unit (kinship), to race, language, regional, and religious groups, or to a host of other social groups.[7] By contrast, strong attachments to the "nation" (the concept may sometimes be difficult to imagine) and its political institutions and symbols may be feeble or entirely absent; national institutions may seem alien, foreign, or irrelevant to oneself. Among other things, this means that political loyalties will often be so weakened that the government will seem illegitimate in the eyes of many individuals ostensibly included as "citizens" of the country. Moreover, there will probably be strong resistance to efforts by national leaders to replace these parochial loyalties with obligations to national institutions, particularly when the obligations include duties considered distasteful or unnecessary. In these situations, national identifications must *compete* with parochial ones for an individual's allegiance. In many nations, the loss of parochial identifications may seem extremely threatening because it appears to destroy one's social identity. One observer explains:

To subordinate parochial identifications in favor of a generalized commitment to an over arching and somewhat alien civil order is to risk a loss of definition as an autonomous person, either through absorption or a culturally undifferentiated mass, or, what is even worse, through domination by some other rival ethnic, racial or linguistic community that is able to imbue that order with the temper of its own personality.[8]

At the same time, so long as these parochial loyalties predominate within a society its people cannot be said to belong to a nation in any psychological sense; the political culture, in effect, will be oriented mostly around identifications and obligations to subnational units.

In many fragmented cultures, one finds some social groups with strong regime loyalties while others are largely parochialistic; this unevenness of national identification is a fertile spawning ground for civil wars, coups, and other demonstrations of rebellion against established political authority, and of conflicts between those seeking to keep others within the national political system and those seeking to escape its embrace.

2. *The lack of widely accepted and operative civil procedures for conflict management.* States with fragmented political cultures have a tendency toward widespread political violence, chronically unreconciled conflicts of great intensity among major social groups, and general deviation from the orderly, civil procedures found in more stable systems. The rules of the game through which politics are actually conducted (and, frequently, the subjective rules preferred by many citizens) are likely to be quite at variance with the official norms of the society insofar as the official norms stress order in conflict management. In many developing nations, the failure of civil procedures for conflict resolution stems from a widespread inability to accept the idea that political conflicts should be resolved according to abstract rules, enforced through national political institutions, and based on more or less impersonal standards; rather, traditional modes of conflict resolution derived from tribal or regional custom, prenational political institutions, or other sources are preferred. Especially when the legitimacy and authority of the institutions enforcing civil order are themselves in considerable doubt—when

the right of those administering the rules to enforce them is challenged—a willingness to "play by the rules" is often absent; such polities lack legitimating symbols that will give civil procedures acceptance among the masses.

Whenever the legitimacy of the political institutions charged with conflict management is challenged, whether in a developed or developing nation, one would expect conflict management to be increasingly difficult. But the developing nations, especially, face the problem of conflict management almost routinely because of the particular conditions associated with their transition from colonial to postcolonial status. The scale and volume of political disagreement among social groups is likely to be very high because basic understandings for the government of civil affairs have to be created; almost all the rules of the game are potentially at issue and all groups are politically threatened. Further, new rules and rulers derived from a national government are bound to collide with other rules: local government officials must contend with tribal and clan leaders, reforming governmental economists with tradition-bound landowners, the older generation with the younger, and so forth. Also, the process of creating political order is permeated with tension, dislocation, and threat because the foundations of social life are often shaken, with a consequent heightening of anxieties and hostilities that may easily spill into political affairs. Notes one observer:

> In all the transitional societies people are going through a profound process of psychological adjustment as their old social order is disrupted and the relationships of family, tribe, clan and village are upset and new patterns are emerging. These psychological disruptions can create deep feelings of ambivalence and uncertainty and can inhibit all effective action and stimulate widespread feelings of anxiety and alienation.[9]

Political violence and disagreement over civil rules are never absent in any political system, of course; the distinction between the political turmoil of fragmented and integrated political cultures lies in the pervasiveness of disorder, the lack of consensus on rules for peaceful conflict management, and the duration of these problems in the fragmented cultures.

3. *The prevalence of political distrust between social groups.*
In fragmented political cultures, political distrust toward other
social groups, sometimes verging upon a social paranoia, is often
so endemic that virtually all major socio-economic groups experience it. This social hostility is often the genesis of civil disorders, governmental instability, and other political problems
commonly identified with fragmented cultures. The constant reoc-
currence of political disorders involving deep group animosities
tends to reinforce the existing political hostilities and, hence,
group distrust becomes both cause and consequence of political
instability in many fragmented cultures. While the basis of intense distrust between major social groupings often has deep
historical, economic, or religious and ethnic roots, the sentiment
commonly involves a conviction that others wish to deprive one's
own social group of political liberties, economic advantages, or
historically enjoyed social privileges; therefore, the political
ascendency of other groups, through control of political or economic institutions, would be detrimental to one's own social
group. There may even be a belief that other groups intend to
destroy, imprison, or banish one from the nation.

This pattern of widespread distrust, once established, tends to
be inherited by new generations through their own political socialization. As this occurs, the conflict problem can become almost intractable, because it is woven into the historical consciousness of major social groups. Moreover, in political communities
characterized by the conflict problem, the political arts associated
with more peaceful conflict resolution—bargaining, compromise,
delayed gratification, social tolerance, and a consensus on certain
fundamental social issues—are not likely to be highly prized by
many political leaders, parties, or organizations. Often, therefore,
the national government can maintain civic order and national
authority only by force and by the suppression of conflicts without their satisfactory resolution; conflicts then simmer just below
the surface of visibility, capable of erupting in sudden and un-
expected ways, or of adding additional intensity and difficulty to
the handling of the most necessary, routine forms of civic life.

4. *National governments tend to be unstable in form and duration.* It is hardly surprising that fragmented political cultures are

so often found with precarious national government structures; the conditions for stable, durable national government are usually absent or weak. In general, the prevalence of widespread parochial loyalties in fragmented cultures means that attachments to national government institutions are weak or wavering, and that no broad consensus on the form of government may exist. Moreover, group hostilities, together with the absence of a traditional acceptance of peaceful conflict management, may mean that the real or alleged triumph of one political party or faction at the national level may be the signal for open rebellion and mass disorder among those factions which feel most threatened. Newly established national governments may find it difficult to rule through consensus, freely competitive elections, and other procedures common to democracy; often, such governments begin by espousing broad civil liberties, public participation in political life, party competition, and other attributes of democracy, but then find that political disorder becomes chronic. Soon, the government becomes increasingly autocratic and nondemocratic as a justification for preserving civic order; this may, in turn, lead to the political repression of the regime's most vigorous critics, who become the nuclei for further rebellion against the regime. In less extreme cases, governmental instability in fragmented cultures may appear as a constant change of party majorities controlling the government or as a succession of new "strong men"; in more extreme cases, the form of government itself may be changed frequently as one new faction succeeds another in control of the national apparatus. This leads to a succession of constitutions and, quite often, further instability. In short, governmental instability is both cause and result of the other conditions we have mentioned.

Many experts would extend or qualify this list in some manner but it does capture, at least, the essentials of a fragmented culture and suggests how they frustrate the task of nation building. Nonetheless, many states continue to exist in spite of their fragmented cultures, albeit with a fragile civic order prone to the turmoil we associate with fragmentation. The continued existence of these states can be illustrated by a brief examination of several older nations with fragmented cultures—a reminder, as well, that cultural fragmentation is not confined solely to the newer African and Asian states.

Fragmented Cultures in Older States. Extreme cultural fragmentation is less common among the older states of Europe, the British Empire, and North America than among the African and Asian countries. One reason is that the stress and conflict usually inherent in nation building were often confronted and resolved centuries earlier, though not without considerable bloodshed, prolonged turmoil, and a large degree of instability in national boundaries and regimes. Many modern states, entering the twentieth century afflicted by extreme fragmentation (like the old Austro-Hungarian Empire, once a European landmark), have disintegrated into secessionist states or have been absorbed, willingly or otherwise, into other states (Serbia and Latvia, for example), or have been forced (like Czechoslovakia) into close political collaboration with a major power. However, many of the fragmentation problems in the European states have been more or less settled by expulsion or elimination of dissident minorities; Poland's major minorities, once accounting for one-third of the total national population, were decimated by the murder and expulsion of most Jews during World War II and by the subsequent repatriation of 9 million Germans. Most European states are more homogeneous today due to similar persecution and flight of minorities, a reminder that the coexistence of cultural diversity and political liberty within the same nation is uneasy indeed.

Fragmented political cultures, nonetheless, still exist in developed nations. There is considerable evidence that nationalist sentiments, combined with simmering anti-Soviet animosity, still smoulder among sizable portions of the populations of Poland, Czechoslovakia, Hungary, and other Soviet-dominated European nations; in these countries, ambivalence or hostility to the dominant Soviet-backed regimes, together with considerable aversion to the ideological and political rules of the game instituted by the Soviets, have occasionally flamed into open rebellion—as in Hungary (1956) and Czechoslovakia (1968)—but the swift, brutal, and effective suppression of both insurrections apparently smothered much of this nationalist sentiment, forcing the populations to make their peace with the new order.

Today, the most dangerously fragmented political culture in Europe is Northern Ireland's, where internal tension has flared into a chronic civil war. At the root of the violence are numerous political cleavages, overlaid and intensified by a profound religious schism of historic proportions.[10] The current civil violence began in 1968, but its origins are centuries old. In the seventeenth century Ireland's native, largely Catholic, population lost its political and economic autonomy, together with much of its social ascendancy, to English settlers who ruled the island in the name of Protestantism and the British Empire. Centuries of intermittent civil violence and uneasy peace followed as the native Catholic majority sought to reassert its control; finally, a prolonged civil war, begun at the turn of the century, culminated in 1920 with the establishment of the predominantly Catholic, autonomous Irish Free State, embracing most of the island and its population; eventually, the Irish Free State (now Eire) seceded from the British Commonwealth. But the six counties of Northern Ireland, containing about a million and a half people predominantly Protestant and English in their loyalties, formed the state of Northern Ireland and continued as a member of the British Commonwealth. This partitioning of the island brought only a fragile peace to the northern counties. The Protestant-dominated Unionist Party, controlling the government in Belfast, has (with the support of the Protestant majority) tolerated and often abetted discrimination against the one-third of their countrymen who are Catholic; in particular, Catholics have been largely forced into the lower classes by discrimination in employment, housing, education, and the civil service; in Londonderry, where a Catholic majority existed, electoral laws were rigged to assure a Protestant majority in the local government. Protestants, largely regarding the Catholic minority as a dangerous and alien presence, suspect that Catholics wish ill to the new nation and hope to force a union with the Catholic-dominated government in Dublin; this, in turn, fires an intense animosity toward the Dublin government, which has been suspected of instigating armed revolt against the Protestant government and of harboring revolutionaries escaping from the North. The Catholic minority, without full civil rights and frustrated by decades of apparently futile protest, looks upon the Belfast government as a conspirator with London in a strategy of suppressing the Catholic opposition. These conflicts are superimposed upon historic grievances: memories of historic persecutions and violence on both sides; Protestant bitterness over Eire's failure to support England in World War II (it remained neutral), and an abiding fear that Protestants might be forced from the Commonwealth and submerged in a Catholic-dominated state; and Catholic resentment of promises often made, but unfulfilled, by both London and Dublin, to rectify the worst civil deprivation. In short, Northern Ireland today comes closer than any other modern nation to reflecting the lack of regime consensus, the political distrust, and the conflicting political identification so often observed in newly emerging nations.

Until quite recently, France enjoyed an unchallenged reputation as Europe's most fragmented political culture. The deep disorder in French political culture was revealed in its turbulent political history. Since the Great Revolution of 1789, France has experienced five Republics, dominated by liberal and moderate elements (1792, 1848, 1870, 1945, and 1958), four monarchial restorations engineered by the Right (1804, 1815, 1830, 1852), numerous hybrid governments, and thirteen different constitutions —all, until recently, afflicted by the instability and transiency which have been the preeminent characteristics of French government for nearly two centuries. Behind this chronic political derangement lie deep cleavages in French political culture. To begin, in a very important sense the French never settled the Revolution of 1789 by achieving a lasting consensus between republican and anti-republican elements in the population over the form and philosophy of national government. The failure of the anti-republican elements to accept the Revolution of 1789 left an angry and embittered portion of the population ready to undermine the republican governments and to replace them with rightist, monarchial forms, or their successors, such as the Vichy regime during World War II. This rupture between right and left over the basic political formula was further aggravated because it corresponded to clerical and anti-clerical sentiments occasioned by the Catholic Church. Moreover, within France's liberal, republican elements ran a schism between those who emphasized political liberty and those who wanted economic equality—a division between political liberals and economic level-lers. Then, too, class antagonisms and their political expression are endemic to French civic life, sometimes reinforcing other political divisions. "Divisions run deep in France," summarizes one observer. "They cut across each other and lead to a frag-mentation of the basic social attitudes which accounts for much of the ideological and political sectionalism of the country. There are oppositions between town and country, employer and worker, the provinces and Paris, Church and anti-Church."[11]

Out of this political dissonance arose a characteristic French political style. A multitude of ideologically rigid, deeply divided political parties and factions competed for control of governments or worked for their dissolution. Because political factions es-poused ideologically dogmatic, incompatible concepts of the con-stitutional order, compromise and collaboration between politi-cal groups was very difficult. Political distrust—between parties, social classes, clerical and anti-clerical elements, and other major social groups—reinforced and perpetuated itself, undermining consensus. A mutually accepted concept of political rules of the game could not easily develop, leading factions to suspect the worst when their opposition obtained a measure of political power. These conditions easily led to resort to violence and revo-lution as methods for accomplishing major political change—the "mystique of the barricades" long honored by all elements in French politics. It is hardly surprising, under these conditions, that the path of French history is strewn with abandoned con-stitutions, overturned governments, and violence. More remark-able is the apparent attainment of a previously unknown political stability in the aftermath of de Gaulle's seizure of the government in 1958 and the subsequent creation of the Fifth Republic, which has shown more durability than most observers would have pre-dicted. It may be, as many interpreters have argued, that the old divisions within the political culture are slowly disappearing. Class antagonisms may be blunted by growing social mobility and economic equality, the regional culture gradually weakening under the impact of national television, new population mobility, and mass education.[12] As France gradually achieves full indus-trialization and the peasantry—traditionally the backbone of

French culture—slowly disappears, many bitter conflicts between capital and labor, province and city can fade. Beyond this, a new pragmatism and ideological moderation may be emerging among the younger leaders of the nation. But many observers, aware of the nation's long history of political fragmentation and the depth of past political cleavages, prefer to leave judgment suspended concerning the future.

Illustrations only hint at the complex repercussions which take place in a society where a fragmented political culture prevails. But such a discussion should illuminate why cultural fragmentation and national political instability coexist and why such fragmentation occupies the constant attention of scholars and statesmen concerned with creating and maintaining political order in the world.

POLITICAL INTEGRATION

Like the term "political fragmentation," the concept of a politically *integrated* culture has been interpreted in different ways. Fortunately, a convergence of ideas about the major characteristics of an integrated political culture has resulted in the widespread use of this term to discuss, in particular, the older nations of Europe, Anglo-America, and a few non-Western nations.

The Meaning of Integration. In a great many respects, the characteristics of an integrated political culture are the reverse of those we noted earlier in fragmented cultures.[13] Among these characteristics are the following:

1. *Relatively consistent and hierarchical political identifications.* In politically integrated societies the issue of proper priorities in political identification is usually solved in a manner consistent with a vigorous national government. Citizenly sentiments customarily place political identification with the nation and its governmental representation in first place, subordinating identification and commitment to other governments and social groupings when decisions about loyalties have to be made—in political terms, the nation "comes first." This certainly does not mean that parochial loyalties are absent, but it does mean that the question

of which obligation takes precedence is settled. In many integrated systems, a great deal of autonomy is left to local, regional, and state governments, which continue to enjoy the allegiance and commitment of those within their ambit of authority without necessarily forcing a conflict with higher political and governmental domains. But—in sharp contrast to fragmented political cultures—there are seldom social groups or governmental units *competing* for primary loyalties or *succeeding* in such competition. As we shall observe, creating such a hierarchy of sentiments is often arduous and, as the American Civil War testified, may be achieved only after civil disorder and profound constitutional transformation occur; and, pockets of resistance to national identification may remain, as with the French Canadians. Still, for most of the people the order of political allegiance is congruent with the hierarchy of governmental units.

2. *Low levels of political violence and dominance of civil procedures for conflict management.* As one would expect, in integrated societies the basic civic processes are ordinarily peaceful, and widespread, sustained violence is rare. This situation occurs because integrated cultures embrace individuals who have arrived at a fairly high level of political consensus about such fundamental issues as the structure of the national government, the basic procedures for selecting governments, and the proper modes of conflict resolution and other rules of the game; the sort of implacable political animosities which most often trigger political violence are, if not totally eliminated, minimized and buffered by this broad social consensus. In such polities, political conflict tends to center upon questions of policy outputs and inputs to the political system, rather than upon the nature of the system itself. One would expect, as well, to find relatively low levels of political violence associated with widely distributed, rather diffuse political trust between social groupings. Trust of this sort makes civil collaboration and accommodation with other social groups and their political representatives more feasible because there is less suspicion that the political ascendancy of one social interest, or combination of interests, will produce extreme deprivations for others. Quite commonly, highly integrated polities have developed a large number of institutions, particularly polit-

ical parties and styles of political leadership, that emphasize and reward political "brokerage," in which reconciliation of group interests and coalition building among social groups is common; this combination and amalgamation of group demands inhibits the sharp political cleavages between major social groups commonly observed in fragmented cultures. Of course, it is not necessarily true that all societies with low incidence of political violence are integrated (a highly coercive regime may suppress even widespread dissent and disaffection and thereby create an illusory facade of civil peace) but integrated societies, by definition, are low in the violence dimension.

3. *Diffuse political trust among social groups.* Integrated political cultures are often extremely pluralistic (in fact, social pluralism is often greatest among these integrated systems due to the impact of industrialization), yet the widespread political paranoia found among social groups in fragmented societies is generally absent or muted. Why does this social pluralism not produce the deep group tensions found in the fragmented societies? A number of factors seem involved. In part, the variety of formal and informal organizations found in many integrated cultures bring people of different social levels and characteristics together for several common purposes; religious, recreational, occupational, and charitable groups function in this way. This experience of social cooperation often encourages greater social trust and builds common interests, which bridge social cleavages. Often, general education promotes greater social understanding and common cultural experiences. In industrialized economies, there is usually sufficient general prosperity to prevent major social and political issues from developing into struggles between rich and poor in which economic survival for one group or another is at stake. Then, too, in most industrialized societies there is great social mobility and a gradual homogenization of life styles which mutes social differences. Often, a political formula has been created which assures all major social groups an important voice in the political system, or makes it possible for new groups with growing importance to gain access and influence in the system. In any case, one commonly finds, within integrated cultures, that major social groups have found formal and informal tech-

niques for social and political collaboration to the extent that abiding social hostilities are generally absent or comparatively brief.

4. *Reasonably strong and durable regime loyalties.* Within an integrated political culture one expects to find widespread public acceptance of the national form of government and agreement about its legitimacy—that is, people agree upon how their national government should generally function and upon its right to govern. It is in this sense that one speaks of a population having accepted the *constitutional order;* the basic national forms of governmental institutions, the rules by which the political process operates, and the symbols and officials of government have established a firm rooting in public sentiment. In extremely integrated societies, this acceptance may be so profound that the way the political process operates is simply accepted as a "given," something natural and normal, to be accepted as a fundamental social reality removed from the arena of political debate. In all modern nations, including those considered well integrated, one can discover some dissident elements whose allegiance to the constitutional order is absent or weak; levels of allegiance may vary to some degree even among those accepting the political order. Nonetheless, in integrated political cultures the majority of citizens have the most fundamental kind of regime allegiance, a "rain and sunshine" loyalty, the most potent kind of commitment "over and above—in spite of—its [the regime's] performance."[14] One would expect, in cultures with strong regime loyalties, that the authority of the national government would extend broadly and deeply into the society, that its capacity to "penetrate" and "extract" from social groups and resources would be considerable, and that, in general, its dominion would extend with considerable evenness over all the territory incorporated within the state.

Political Integration and the West. Most analysts assert that the majority of politically integrated societies are found in Western Europe and Anglo-America with a scattering of representatives in the Middle East and Asia (principally Japan). These nations are customarily considered the most developed, not only in the political sense of having the most integrated political cultures, but in the sense of having generally modern cultures and highly industrialized economies. Many scholars believe that achieving political integration is almost a prerequisite for polities to develop stable national governments, productive economies, and the ability to assume the attributes of modern Western culture.

The great incidence of integrated cultures in the West may have much to do with the highly industrialized economies of its nations. A very productive economy often encourages political culture integration; and, it inhibits many of the social cleavages and crises that might otherwise arise between major social groups. The collapse of a productive economy may, in fact, produce serious fragmentation in a previously integrated culture. Many commentators have observed, for example, that West Germany's impressive "economic miracle"—its vigorous recovery from the ashes of World War II—has engendered an "ideology of prosperity" among the population. Citizen support for the new West German Government, so the observers suggest, was nourished by widespread satisfaction with economic life. It was comparatively easy for West Germans to accept a virtually new political system when it came so attractively wrapped in industrial prosperity. In the same vein, it has been suggested that the American political culture, often cited as the premier illustration of an integrated system, owes much of its stability to the phenomenally productive American economy. It is not hard for Americans to accept, almost unquestioningly, the virtue of their political institutions and to settle their political differences civilly when they have prospered so well under their system.

It is difficult for a nation with a fragmented political culture to industrialize. For most developing nations, industrialization requires enormous sacrifices from their people; it places the great burden upon the national government of imposing very strict economic and political restraints upon the people to assure that enough of the nation's scarce resources will be poured into industry until satisfactory growth is achieved. In a country deeply divided over allegiance to the national government, where the central government's structure and authority are constantly challenged and debated, this sort of economic management may be impossible. Since a poor, nonindustrialized economy intensifies the social cleavages that frustrate political integration, the bitter circle of cause and effect undermines cultural integration and compounds the task of nation building.

The high incidence of politically integrated cultures among Western nations has many explanations but one reason is that these nations began the task of nation building much earlier than the currently developing countries—in many instances, three centuries earlier; most Western nations, in effect, have largely completed the long process of political integration (Great Britain and the United States) or are well along toward the goal (France and the Soviet Union). Many commentators assert that the path from cultural fragmentation to integration is a progression through a number of specific "phases" or "stages," while other experts assert that such a tidy set of "states" is arbitrary. In any event, the integrated Western societies have become models for the political and economic development of the newer states (understandably, for most of the modernizing elites were educated in the West).

THE CIVIC CULTURE

A different approach to classifying political cultures has been suggested by Gabriel Almond and Sidney Verba in their influential book *The Civic Culture*. Published in 1963, this study is an imaginative, rigorous effort to combine cross-national concepts of political culture with modern techniques of survey research.[15] Almond and Verba's typology of political cultures blends elements of the integrated and fragmented models with other components in political culture literature to produce a distinctive synthesis of ideas and data representing the most ambitious effort to study political culture comparatively. The cutting point of this study is a critical issue in contemporary global politics: To what extent is it possible for developing countries to achieve a political culture which supports a democratic political system? "If we are to come closer to understanding the problems of the diffusion of democratic culture, we have to be able to specify the content of *what* has to be diffused, to develop appropriate measures of it, to discover its quantitative incidence and demographic distribution in countries with a wide range or experience with democracy,"[16] note the authors. Beginning with this premise, the authors examine the political cultures of five developed nations in which democratic polities currently exist—the United States, Great Britain, Germany, Italy, and Mexico—looking for the "attitude and feeling" of the populations toward their respective political orders. Although the bulk of the study is dedicated to examining the political orientations of more than 1,000 individuals studied and interviewed in each nation, the work's most enduring contribution is the concepts developed by the authors for describing and categorizing political cultures.

Dimensions of Political Culture. The authors' approach to political culture is relatively simple in conceptual outline.[17] Essentially, they suggest that individuals within a political system are oriented toward that system in terms of *cognitions* (knowledge and beliefs about the political system, its officials, and its inputs and outputs), *affects* (emotions about the political system, personnel, and performance), and *evaluations* (judgments and opinions of political objects). It is possible, the authors contend, to specify in a general way the "objects" within the system to which an individual can be oriented. These include the system as a whole, its "input objects" (all the individuals, groups, and processes involved in the flow of policy demands on government), the "output objects" (all the components of policy enforcement), and, finally, the self as a political participant (knowledge of one's rights and obligations as a member of the political system and beliefs about how one should participate in political life). Using these basic concepts as building blocks, the writers suggest that one can categorize citizen orientations within a political system according to the ways in which citizenly cognition, affect, and evaluation relate to the different parts of the system. Using a simple figure, illustrated below, the authors match possible patterns of orientation to different objects within a political system and derive three basic kinds of political culture patterns. Reading across a line in Table 2.1 gives a "score" for each type of political culture by indicating to what objects most citizens in that polity will be oriented in some manner. Against this backdrop, Almond and Verba describe each type of political culture in detail:

TABLE 2.1

Types of Political Culture

	System as General Object	Input Objects	Output Objects	Self as Active Participant
Parochial	0	0	0	0
Subject	1	0	1	0
Participant	1	1	1	1

A "0" means that citizens are very weakly oriented, or entirely indifferent to an object, while a "1" indicates strong involvement with that political object.

Parochial Political Culture: "In these societies there are no specialized political roles: headmanship, chieftainship, "shamanship" are diffuse political-economic-religious roles, and for members of these societies the political orientations to those roles are not separated from their social and religious orientations. A parochial orientation involves the comparative absence of expectations of change initiated by the political system. The parochial expects nothing from the political system. Similarly, in the centralized African chiefdoms and kingdoms to which the political cultures would be predominantly parochial."[18]

Subject Political Culture: "There is a high frequency of orientations toward a differentiated political system and toward the output aspects of the system, but orientations toward specifically input objects, and toward the self as an active participant, approach zero. The subject is aware of specialized governmental authority; he is affectively oriented to it, perhaps taking pride in it, perhaps disliking it; and he evaluates it either as legitimate or as not. But the relationship is toward the system on the general level, and toward the output, administrative, or 'downward flow' side of the political system; it is essentially a passive relationship. . . ."[19]

Participant Political Culture: "The members of the society tend to be explicitly oriented to the system as a whole and to both the political and administrative structures and processes: in other words, to both input and output aspects of the political system. Individual members of the participant polity may be favorably or unfavorably oriented toward an 'activist' role of the self in the polity, though their feelings and evaluations of such a role may vary from acceptance to rejection."[20]

Such descriptions represent *pure* types of political culture, quite unlikely to be found in modern societies; rather, one would expect to find a mixture of different orientations within a society, so that actual political cultures will represent a blend of different elements found in the simple typology above. The authors suggest that the mixture of types will have a profound influence upon the ability of a nation to support a democratic system, and—most importantly to their interest—the type of culture mix which a society achieves will largely determine its ability to move from an underdeveloped political system (typified by a purely *parochial* culture) to a modern democratic system (with a preponderance of *participant* orientations within the system). In a broader perspective, the authors offer some ideas about the mix of cultural types congenial to authoritarian, totalitarian, and democratic regimes generally.

The researchers also consider the problem of political instability, which occupies such a large portion of the writing about *integrated* and *fragmented* political cultures. According to the authors, it is possible to explain political stability and instability in terms of the concepts earlier used to describe political systems generally. Any type of pure political culture, according to Almond and Verba, may be scaled on a continuum from *allegiant* to *alienated* depending upon *how* individuals are oriented toward political objects. To illustrate this point, they return to the basic political orientations first mentioned and suggest that these orientations may have a highly positive, neutral, or highly negative character. They suggest (Table 2.2) that political cultures may be *allegiant, apathetic* or *alienated* from the dominant political system according to the quality of these orientations. Under this logic, a subject political culture might be allegiant, apathetic, or alienated. The authors use their survey data to argue, for example, that Great Britain's political culture is both a mixed subject-participant culture and an allegiant one; this means that large portions of the English population should show patterns of political orientation similar to those in the bottom two lines of Table 2.1 and in the first column of Table 2.2. Working with such concepts clearly involves some simplification of reality, for patterns of political culture seldom assume the orderly configurations that precisely fit any of the types developed in Tables 2.1 and 2.2.

TABLE 2.2

Congruence and Incongruence Between Political
Culture and Structure

	Allegiant	*Apathetic*	*Alienated*
Cognitive Orientation	+	+	+
Affective Orientation	+	0	−
Evaluative Orientation	+	0	−

A "+" indicates positive orientation, a "0" indifference, and a "−" a negative (or hostile) orientation.[21]

Nonetheless, these concepts, properly qualified and intelligently interpreted in light of actual data from national populations, provide a very useful working vocabulary for the comparative-government specialist.

The Uses of The Civic Culture. Curiously, the publication of *The Civic Culture* produced no wealth of subsequent elaborations and adaptations of this approach in further research; the authors, themselves, turned to other (though related) matters, and comparative-government specialists seemed content to let the concepts and material rest. Still, the value of *The Civic Culture* must be judged in terms of its potential for further use rather than in terms of its empirical findings alone. Whatever its deficiencies—and they ought to be carefully examined in future research—the Almond and Verba approach provides a set of very useful concepts, together with many hypotheses about how these ideas relate to modern world politics. The framework developed in the book can be applied to problems connected with political development, differences between democratic and nondemocratic political systems, and historical research, as well as contemporary studies. The approach lends itself nicely to sophisticated survey research methods. It offers, further, one of the few cross-cultural approaches to political culture to be empirically tested and refined in the field and ought to inspire future comparative-government specialists to more ambitious effort.

THREE AMONG MANY

The three approaches to political culture we have examined, while common in comparative political literature, are only a few among many approaches. There is no reason to believe that agreement concerning the proper concepts and techniques to be applied to political culture study will soon emerge among comparative political scholars. Further theorizing is certain and the opportunities for research and discovery are abundant. It is important to emphasize, moreover, that the patterns we have described still remain *theories*, which have been partially tested in different national contexts. In effect, we have examined a few of the ideas that constitute the working vocabulary of many comparative political specialists interested in political culture, and we can surely expect further theories to emerge and become part of the literature.

NOTES

1. A useful synopsis of this literature may be found in Myron Weiner, "Political and Social Integration: Forms and Strategies," *The Annals*, 358 (March, 1965), 52–64.
2. See the summary of the developmental elite's role in C. E. Black, *The Dynamics of Modernization* (New York: Harper and Row, 1966), chapter 3.
3. Clifford Geertz (ed.), *Old Societies and New States* (New York: The Free Press, 1963), p. 212.
4. Lucian W. Pye, *Aspects of Political Development* (Boston: Little, Brown, 1966), p. 19.
5. Charles W. Anderson, Fred R. von der Mehden, and Crawford Young, *Issues of Political Development* (Englewood Cliffs, N.J.: Prentice-Hall, 1967), pp. 80–81.
6. *Ibid.*, p. 41.
7. These parochial loyalties, often called "primordial" sentiments, are thoroughly described in Clifford Geertz, "Primordial Sentiments and Civil Politics in the New States," in Clifford Geertz (ed.), *op. cit.*, pp. 108–28.
8. *Ibid.*, p. 109.
9. Pye, *op. cit.*, p. 13.
10. See Richard Rose, *Governing Without Consensus* (Boston: Beacon Press, 1971).
11. Jean Blondel and E. Drexel Godfrey, Jr., *The Government of France* (New York: Thomas Y. Crowell, 1968), p. 23.
12. This argument has been made by, among others, Philip M. Williams, *Crisis and Compromise* (New York: Doubleday, 1966).
13. The literature on integration is summarized in Claude Ake, *A Theory of*

Political Integration (Homewood, Ill.: The Dorsey Press, 1967), chapter 1.

14. Sidney Verba, "Comparative Political Culture," in Lucian W. Pye and Sidney Verba (eds.), *Political Culture and Political Development* (Princeton, N.J.: Princeton University Press, 1965), p. 529.

15. Gabriel Almond and Sidney Verba, *The Civic Culture* (Princeton, N.J.: Princeton University Press, 1963).

16. *Ibid.*, pp. 9–10.

17. *Ibid.*, chapter 1.

18. *Ibid.*, pp. 17–18.

19. *Ibid.*, p. 19.

20. *Ibid.*, p. 19.

21. *Ibid.*, p. 22.

3

POLITICAL INTEGRATION: GREAT BRITAIN AND THE UNITED STATES

Discussions of global political order almost inevitably draw the conclusion that the United States and Great Britain are among the world's most *integrated* political cultures if not uniquely alone in their degree of political stability. To most commentators, such observations seem somewhat trite. Still, familiarity should not diminish the importance of these conclusions even if, upon closer inspection, neither country has quite achieved a completely integrated culture. For, in comparative terms, Great Britain and the United States are embodiments of the historical-political continuity and civic stability singularly lacking in a world permeated with political violence and national disorders. It is appropriate, and perhaps unavoidable, that an illustration of political integration should draw upon these two nations.

Great Britain and the United States share much—including a common cultural heritage, a highly industrialized economy, the experience of world power, and democratic political orders—but it is the often striking disparities between the nations which make a comparison of their political cultures, particularly their attainment of political integration under very divergent conditions, so interesting. Great Britain, for example, is an extremely old nation —"old" in any sense of the word; it has maintained its political continuity and identity for more than five hundred years in all conditions from feast to virtual ruin. The United States, though it will observe its bicentennial in this decade, is still a new country where, as many foreign observers have perceptively noted, "history" has little transcendent importance. The United States is, by British standards, a remarkably pluralistic nation, whose ethnic, racial, religious, and regional divisions—to say nothing of its occupational differentiation—exceed anything familiar to the average Briton. Britain's political stability has endured the ascent to empire and the long, agonizing slide into the shadow of the United States; on the other hand, Americans have enjoyed political stability with virtually uninterrupted growth in national prosperity and international power. Such contrasts could continue indefinitely; suffice it to say that political integration was not the result of largely parallel developments in largely similar polities.

Many of the comparative factors will become more meaningful if we examine each nation in turn, beginning in each case with preliminary comments upon the socio-economic setting of the political cultures and then examining these cultures in terms of dimensions we have described earlier.

GREAT BRITAIN

The British have developed a talent for absorbing needed social innovation, often with profound consequences, into the fabric of their traditional political and social orders. In this way problems of continuity and change, so often confounding to other national regimes, have been largely managed; in English terms, it is the business of "muddling through." Consequently, British political life and culture, like other facets of the English nation, are a blend of modernity and tradition evolving within a national setting where a strong sense of community and civic consensus prevail.

An Old Nation. For most practical purposes, Great Britain had achieved, by the end of the eighteenth century, all the vestments of a modern nation, including a strong central government, well-defined national borders, a largely allegiant population, and an increasingly vigorous economy (which greatly enhanced the extractive and allocative powers of the central government).[1] Separated from mainland Europe by a sea which was both an avenue of commerce and a moat against aggressors, the British developed a strong sense of national identity, heightened by their insularity and safety from invasion (the island has not been successfully invaded since 1066). The British think of themselves as a "race" distinctively English, not European—though France is easily visible from Dover on a clear day. This pervasive sense of national identity, a solid bulwark upon which to erect the scaffolding of national government, is enhanced by cultural homogeneity. The nation is more than 95 per cent white, overwhelmingly Protestant and English-speaking, almost entirely Anglo-Saxon, and largely free of the social cleavages which produce the intense parochial loyalties so disruptive to political order in many newer nations. Despite the existence of a state church (Anglican), there is great religious tolerance; the church is customarily outside the ambit of political controversy. While nationalistic stirrings occur fitfully among Scots, Welsh, and Catholics in Northern Ireland, there are no serious secessionist movements within a nation which remains united, as it has been historically, by allegiance to the Crown.

Most of Britain's explosive social controversies and politically significant transformations took place after her national identity, political order, and culture were largely established. In a society where the political culture nourished a style of leadership emphasizing moderation, accommodation, and experimentalism, change could proceed in a setting favorable to adaptation and moderation. Industrialization, with all its complex economic and political ramifications, was absorbed into the culture by the end of the eighteenth century without widespread political dislocations. The right to vote was gradually extended during the eighteenth and nineteenth centuries, first to the rising middle class spawned by industrialization, and then to the working classes. The severe economic retrenchment forced upon Britain by World War II and her loss of empire were accepted by both major parties; the gradual transition to the welfare state was similarly accepted, if not welcomed. This is not to suggest that Britain's major social transitions were effected without considerable political debate, conflict, and sometimes disorder; but they were made, and absorbed into the fabric of the national political consensus, in fairly short order.

Regime Orientation. Great Britain, unlike the United States, has no single document defining its fundamental governmental structures and processes as the American Constitution does. Nonetheless, one speaks routinely of the British "Constitution." This "Constitution" is actually a collection of documents that appeared at different times over the last five centuries, together with a set of unwritten but broadly distributed and deeply held public convictions about the proper scope and conduct of government. These documents and public sentiments are so pervasively understood and accepted that they have the force of constitutional law and the power of tradition. This, in itself, is strong testimony to the strength and durability of political consensus in Great Britain. Thus, the major parties have divided over public policy but not over this "constitutional" framework. The irreparable social cleavages produced by disagreements over the legitimacy or form of the national government that so often afflict fragmented political cultures have been almost alien to Great Britain in modern times. The monarch in Bagehot's famous phrase, "reigns but does not rule," yet the monarchy is not an antique and irrelevant institution; it has served as a symbol of continuity and unity to the British public, a repository of patriotic sentiment above parliamentary conflict and partisan squabbles, hence, a rallying point among people often divided on many other political matters.[2]

Traditionally, pride and respect for the national regime have been remarkably high in Great Britain. This broadly dispersed citizen support is reflected in a comparative study, conducted in the early 1960's, which listed the aspects of their culture that respondents in five nations spontaneously mentioned as sources of particular pride; these responses are summarized in Table 3.1. According to the British sample, political structures and social legislation were widely admired. The difference, in this respect, between Great Britain and the United States, in one group, and the other nations with considerably less evidence of regime admiration is striking.

Although studies suggest that regime support is strongest among the more affluent segments of English society, the sentiment is widely distributed among virtually all social groups. Particularly since the partition of Ireland in 1922 removed the one significant secessionist population remaining within the British

Political Culture

TABLE 3.1

Aspects of Nation in Which Respondents Report Pride,
by Nation, 1960

Percentage who say they are proud of	U.S.	U.K.	Germany	Italy	Mexico
Governmental, political institutions	85	46	7	3	30
Social legislation	13	18	6	1	2
Position in international affairs	5	11	5	2	3
Economic system	23	10	33	3	24
Characteristics of people	7	18	36	11	15
Spiritual virtues and religion	3	1	3	6	8
Contributions to the arts	1	6	11	16	9
Contributions to science	3	7	12	3	1
Physical attributes of country	5	10	17	25	22
Nothing or don't know	4	10	15	27	16
Other	9	11	3	21	14
Total % of responses*	158	148	148	118	144
Total % of respondents	100	100	100	100	100
Total number of cases	970	963	955	995	1,007

* Percentages exceed one hundred of multiple responses.
SOURCE: Gabriel Almond and Sidney Verba, *The Civic Culture*, p. 102.

Isles, demands for major constitutional changes have been extremely rare. However, as we shall remark later, the traditional
public support for Britain's major political institutions has been
severely tested in the 1960's and 1970's by growing economic
stagnation and a recessive economy, by a lackluster foreign policy, and by general austerity aggravated by the extreme dislocations in the wake of the energy crisis in the mid-1970's. Given sufficient time, such continual crises may be the water that wears
away the rock of public confidence.

Political Trust. Britain has a long history of citizen trust in
government and in other Englishmen. In part, this trust reflects
the constitutional consensus of the nation's major parties; though
majority parties wax and wane, the opposition does not fear a major constitutional reconstruction or radical policy departure of the

type that customarily triggers strong suspicion between partisan groups. Moreover, citizen trust has been sufficiently firm to permit governments a very great measure of privacy in conducting their business; leaders have been expected to deliberate and decide public policy without constant public disclosure, and the British civil service is tightly sealed from the prying of the press— a situation that has been understood by all concerned as the way things are done.

Citizen trust has also been reflected in relatively low levels of hostility between partisans of the nation's major parties and in the widely pervasive evidence of social collaboration and openness in English society. Intensely partisan Conservatives and Labourites can often be antagonists, of course, but there does not seem to be any widely shared polarization of feeling between the followers of the two parties. One interesting example of this can be found in Almond and Verba's study of British attitudes toward intermarriage with a member of a different political faith. The authors found that the great majority of respondents, on both

TABLE 3.2

Social Trust and Distrust, by Nation, 1960

Percentage who agree that	U.S.	U.K.	Germany	Italy	Mexico
Statements of Distrust					
"No one is going to care much what happens to you, when you get right down to it."	38	45	72	61	78
"If you don't watch yourself, people will take advantage of you."	68	75	81	73	94
Statements of Trust					
"Most people can be trusted."	55	49	19	7	30
"Most people are more inclined to help others than to think of themselves first."	31	28	15	5	15
"Human nature is fundamentally cooperative."	80	84	58	55	82
Total number of respondents	970	963	955	995	1,007

SOURCE: Gabriel Almond and Sidney Verba, *The Civic Culture*, p. 267.

Conservative and Labourite sides, might not vote for the other party but were indifferent to the prospect of inheriting a relative who did.[3] A more general indication of civic trust can be found in Table 3.2 which indicates citizen responses to several questions asked in the five-nation study. Comparatively, the British scored at the higher ends of the scale on civic trust and the lower ends on political distrust.

Membership in secondary groups is not as frequent among English as Americans (roughly 60 per cent of Americans belong, compared to 50 per cent of Britons), but it is widely distributed and politically significant. Many social scientists assert that experience of voluntary group activity often encourages a strong sense of political efficacy and competence among individuals. Such activity provides experience in social interaction and an awareness of other individual and group viewpoints, as well as encouraging skills with considerable political applicability. The prevalence of group activism among the British appears to suggest a public with a substantial sense of civic competence, trust in collaborative activity, and interest in social affairs.

Rules of the Game. Britain's political culture is too richly complex to reduce to simple formulas, yet the elements essential to its character are few. In particular, four words describe the dominant values that have set the cultural pattern: *deference, liberty, moderation,* and *continuity.*

Most Britons have accepted social inequalities as a natural, even proper, facet of life; with this has developed what is commonly called *deference* in British social and political life. Deference, according to Bagehot, is a natural acceptance of one's betters: "Certain persons are by common consent agreed to be wiser than others, and their opinion is, by consent, to rank for much more than its numerical value. We may in these happy nations weigh votes as well as count them."[4] Deference in Britain has traditionally gone to those who sit high on the social ladder by virtue of wealth, birth, and education. In political terms, it has meant a general acceptance of the right of the upper classes to run political affairs, with respect for the public will, but with a great latitude for independence, on the assumption that the public will customarily defer to their judgment. "Leaders in political life," says Richard Rose, "are expected to be uncommon men and enjoy deference on that basis. National politics is primarily for those who have been born to a high station in life, or have qualified for a high station by youthful educational achievement."[5] One consequence of this deference is that most Britons feel no obligation to participate actively and vociferously in public life. In a typical finding, Butler and Stokes estimated in 1964 that, while 77 per cent of the British population voted in general elections, only about 8 per cent attended political meetings, and only 3 per cent actively participated in the campaigns; moreover, only 25 per cent of the population appeared to be even nominal party members.[6] Widespread deference also means that the British do not necessarily gauge the acceptability of governmental policy by the extent to which it results from massive interaction between rulers and ruled. Politics, in short, has been considered the rightful vocation of the privileged few, with the occasional participation of the many—an attitude that would be untenable in a system without a high degree of traditional trust. Thus, Butler and Stokes also discovered that a majority of British citizens believed elections and political parties made the government pay attention to public opinion, but well over half also believed the government often paid little attention to public opinion—still, this appeared neither to surprise nor to irritate most respondents.[7]

Britons esteem *political liberties* highly; expressive and participatory freedom is, and has been, extensive in England. Indeed, the freedom of political dissent and the legitimacy of criticism of political leaders are deeply etched in political practice as, for example, in the assumption that there can be no proper "government" (in the sense of a ruling majority party in Parliament) without an opposition; hence, the Crown pays the salary of the "Leader of the Opposition"—who, significantly, is known officially as the Leader of the *Loyal* Opposition—and Parliament is so arranged that Government and Opposition parties face each other to emphasize a necessary dualism between responsibility and criticism. Although there is a state church, there has been no significant harassment of "nonconformist" denominations for more than a century. Although Britons, as we have seen, do not esteem participatory democracy as highly as Americans, opportunities for a wide range of political activities have been available to the average Briton, and other evidence of expressive freedom, such as a vigorous free press, is abundant.

Continuity in British politics has been possible, in good measure, because of *moderation* in national leadership styles. The logic of British leadership style has been to mix new policy and institutions in such a way that the old can be preserved—at least in form, if not in substance—while the necessary modernization is achieved. Thus, the gradual weakening of the monarchy to largely symbolic status and the displacement of true governmental power to Parliament was achieved without abolishing the monarchy; the House of Lords, similarly, remains, but largely ceases to govern. So, too, in matters of policy. Although the British Labour Party has often spoken in the hard-line ideological rhetoric of socialism and seemed, before World War II, to be quite separated, if not polarized, from the Conservatives on most policy issues, when Labour achieved clear parliamentary control in 1945 and in the years thereafter, it followed a moderate, pragmatic social policy, inspired by socialism yet sensitive to the need to make concessions to the Conservative viewpoint. British political leaders are customarily pragmatists and bargainers, innovators rather than revolutionaries, men who largely distrust the rigidities of ideological thinking (even if they occasionally borrow the vocabulary) and who are committed to change within the context of respect for tradition.

Political Competence and Efficacy. Numerous studies reveal that Britons generally demonstrate a strong sense of political competence and political efficacy. The majority of Britons, for instance, customarily report a conviction that they can do something to influence national and local laws, and that they follow political news and discuss it to some extent.[8] However, this belief and interest is not accompanied by an equally strong feeling of obligation to participate actively in political life; the deference so often noted in citizenly attitudes toward political business apparently diminishes the conviction that one ought to attend to political matters oneself. This does not imply apathy. Britons commonly express a conviction that an individual ought to be active in community life in some manner, and most of them are, in some way, involved in the group life of their community. Still, the British as a nation do not share with their American cousins the conviction that vigorous and repeated civic involvement at all levels (particularly, in national affairs) is the mark of a truly conscientious citizen.

Part of the high level of British civic competence and efficacy may be attributed to the physical character of the British isles. Britain is a small nation of 50 million people living on an island little more than 500 miles from north to south and seldom more than 150 miles wide—an area somewhat larger than the state of Florida. London, the political, economic and cultural center of the nation, is both physically and psychologically close to almost all Englishmen, so that major political events never seem remote, nor government distant. Then, too, Britain is a modern nation where political news is readily and continually available through all the media. Local governmental institutions have functioned for centuries. All of which, in different ways, would seem likely to heighten awareness of political affairs and encourage democratic participation when it is expected.

A Fading Splendor? Notwithstanding all that has been written about the massive, almost singular, British political consensus, the fading of empire and the slow decline into a gray mid-century of political and economic mediocrity may be eating away the historic British confidence in government, leadership, and Crown. Gathering evidence suggests that significant portions of the British public may have become disenchanted with the worth and effectiveness of their governmental institutions. A 1967 poll, for instance, revealed that 58 per cent of a sample English public agreed that "Britain is a third-class power nowadays," and 65 per cent accepted the proposition that "Foreigners don't pay as much attention to Britain as they used to."[9] Most significantly, perhaps, the youngest portion of the adult respondents were the most likely to agree with both suggestions.

The erosion of confidence in British political institutions was also revealed in a recent study concerning the political attitudes of British children between eight and seventeen years old. In one segment, the youngsters were asked how they felt about the statement "Britain is the best country in the world"; almost half

TABLE 3.3

Objects of National Pride Among
British School Children, 1968

	Age		
	8–10	11–13	14–17
Percentage who say they are proud of	(N=140)	(N=203)	(N=189)
Governmental, political institutions	19%	20%	30%
Social legislation	1	2	3
Position in international affairs*	4	7	8
Economic system	3	6	7
Characteristics of the people	3	3	9
Spiritual virtues and religion	1	–	–
Contributions to the arts†	10	10	6
Contributions to science	4	3	1
Physical attributes of country	2	6	4
Nothing or don't know	21	10	10
Other (general quality of life,‡	17	30	21 ⎫
history, glorious past,	9	9	12 ⎬
other)	5	4	5 ⎭
Total	99%	110%	116%

* Includes foreign policy in present study.

† Includes educational system, "literacy" in the present study.

‡ Sports, fashion, pop groups, etc.

SOURCE: Jack Dennis, Leon Lindberg, and Donald McCrone, "Support for Nation and Government Among English School Children," *British Journal of Political Science*, I, pt. 1 (January, 1971), 33. Slightly adapted.

(46 per cent) expressed moderate to strong disagreement—a surprisingly large portion in a nation where public confidence in government has been very high and the young might be expected to express strong patriotic sentiments due to their early political socialization. The extent to which government was a source of pride among the school children is suggested in Table 3.3, which indicates that government, while the most frequently mentioned item, was selected by less than one-third of the children in the most politically affirmative age group.

It would be premature to assume that such fragmentary evidence indicates a truly pervasive weakening of the political integration in one of the world's most durable political orders. At the same time, such data is a reminder of the extreme political stress experienced by the English since World War II, a situation likely to cause some critical reappraisals among citizens in any nation similarly affected. In a broader perspective, citizen allegiance to national political structures may be considerably easier to create and maintain during a period of growing prosperity and political success at home and abroad—the sort of experience enjoyed by Britons through World War I and by Americans through the middle of the century. Political consensus, in such cases, may rest upon economic productivity, with its generally benign political consequences. In any case, Britain's decline to a second-rate world power, for whatever reasons, will test severely the mettle of the British political consensus.

THE UNITED STATES

The United States is in sharp contrast to Great Britain geographically and socially. Unlike the insular, socially homogeneous British, Americans are a continental, socially diversified people. Americans live in the fourth-largest nation in the world by size and population—approximately 207 million people occupying more than 3.5 million square miles of territory, including some of the richest natural resources enjoyed by any people.

Not only the vastness but the social mixture of the United States frequently surprises foreign visitors. One in every ten Americans is black; one in every twenty, Spanish-American; there are sizable native Indian and Oriental groups, as well as a considerable scattering of other racial types. At least half the present population traces its origin to English, German, Irish, Italian, or other nonnative antecedents, a reminder of the more than 45 million immigrants who entered American society since 1820. Not surprisingly, there is religious diversity. The three major religious communities—Protestant, Catholic, and Jewish—each embrace a multitude of different credal groups, including more than fifty major Protestant denominations alone. Added to this social and religious diversity has been a variety of regional subcultures, most graphically represented by the South, where parochial political and social outlooks have only slowly dissolved as a truly national culture emerges. If, to these differences, are added those created by occupational differentiations, the true heterogeneity of the American population can be appreciated.

This social diversity has affected the political culture in many ways. It has undoubtedly added emphasis and urgency to certain values long maintained as part of the American political credo, particularly social tolerance, equality of opportunity, political freedom, and other values that make possible a political community among diverse social groups. It has also encouraged a political style, among leaders, in which the dominant techniques tend to be bargaining, compromise, nonideological stances, and other attitudes that encourage the aggregation and harmonization of competing social demands upon government. The "civil war potential" among competing social interests can rise dangerously high. Almost all major social groups sometimes find themselves in competition with, or in opposition to, other interests over economic and political objectives. In this environment, groups often seek to maximize their political influence and to counter the influence of opposition groups through the formation of various organized interest groups (or "secondary associations"), which marshal individual resources, coordinate leadership, and direct political effort through collective action. Nowhere else in the world have these interest groups multiplied to the extent found in the United States. While the open and extensive *lobbying* of government is their most distinctive activity, these interest groups undertake a wealth of other tasks.

Social diversity also means the existence of many subcultures, particularly racial and ethnic, in which political orientations divergent from, and sometimes hostile to, the dominant political culture develop. These subcultures are especially likely to be in conflict with the dominant culture when social groups have been the object of political discrimination. The most violent eruption of subcultural tension was the American Civil War of 1860–65 when, in effect, a secessionist region espousing a confederate philosophy of national political institutions attempted to forcibly dissolve the political compact with the remainder of the nation that held a federal conception of national government. The philosophical argument, growing from social and economic differences between the two regions, was settled militarily; such a fundamental constitutional cleavage has not reoccurred. However, large numbers of blacks and native Indians, especially, continue to express diminished confidence and allegiance toward the dominant national political institutions and political culture. Civil rights continue to be a major national issue in good measure because many blacks, Indians, and other minorities feel that they have not been accorded the opportunities and political rights enjoyed by the dominant racial groups within the population—in short, that they have been excluded from the dominant political culture.

At the same time, many aspects of American society have eased the problem of creating an integrated political culture.[10] The enormously productive American economy has distributed wealth and comfort widely, giving the majority of Americans the highest standard of living in the world and encouraging a sense of satisfaction and optimism with social affairs. Moreover, economic productivity has meant social mobility and an opportunity for many disadvantaged groups to get a "piece of the pie" economically, thereby lessening political and social disaffection even among the relatively disadvantaged. Then, too, a productive economy fosters group conflicts over governmental resources in which the satisfaction of one side is not necessarily at the expense of the other; it has been possible to satisfy a great variety of competing demands by simply increasing the size of the governmental pie to be divided among competing claimants for favors (through increasing direct and indirect governmental means of diverting social resources to those demanding them).

Many of the fundamental causes of political fragmentation were, in any case, absent when the United States began its own postcolonial development. The nation survived the Revolutionary War with a national government intact, with a population more socially homogeneous than it would ever be again, and with a common language and culture. The Revolution, additionally, had not been a social upheaval; the social elite wielding political power before the Revolution were firmly in control afterward. Also, as many commentators have observed, the United States began its national evolution without an aristocracy to impede its democratization and, consequently, without the provocation for a civil war among classes that left such enduring scars on the political cultures of many other nations. The frontier was an important outlet for social dissidents, a constant incentive for national growth, and a rich resource base for industrialization. Given these advantages, together with the protection afforded by two oceans and by two weak nations on the other borders, the new American nation had both the time and the resources to grow into an integrated political culture although—as the Civil War reminds us—not without many crises in nation building.

The political culture emerging from this social and historical background is not one of "great consensus," though this is so often assumed to be the hallmark of American political opinion. Americans, to be sure, seem largely agreed upon how political affairs should be conducted, but this has not been an agreement uniformly shared among all major social groups nor constant through time. There are many contradictions and inconsistencies in political orientations.

Regime Orientations. Americans have customarily voiced considerable satsifaction with their government and political system, as Table 3.1 suggested by indicating that 85 per cent of the American sample in the five-nation study had spontaneously mentioned their government as a source of pride. This esteem is suggested again by Table 3.4, which assesses regime support in mid-1972, a time when political scandals had obviously caused some public disillusion. Although the proportion expressing dissatis-

TABLE 3.4

Public Regime Support in the United States, 1972

	National Opinion Sample
"Do we need a change in our form of government?"	(N=1106)
Need big change, some change	41.1%
Keep it as is	58.7
Pride in government:	
"I am proud of many things about our system of government."	86.0
(or)	
"I can't find much in our system of government to be proud of."	14.0

SOURCE: Jack Citrin, Herbert McClosky, J. Merrill Shanks, and Paul M. Sniderman, "Personal and Political Sources of Political Alienation" (Paper delivered at the meeting of the American Political Science Association, New Orleans, Louisiana, September 4–9, 1973), p. 11.

faction here is somewhat higher than customarily revealed in such polls (and may only be temporary), it does emphasize that support for the regime is, and probably always has been, somewhat qualified. Blacks and other minority groups often voice more reservations about the regime than do white Americans and the more advantaged generally. In one recent study, almost all of a representative sample of white Americans reported that they expected fair and impartial treatment from government officials, but less than half the black respondents answered similarly. In another study of political cynicism, more than twice as many blacks reported extreme alienation from the political system as did whites. These findings reveal the pattern of diminished regime confidence typical of most studies of black and white political attitudes.[11] Nonetheless, the dominant American mood has traditionally been strong regime support extending broadly across the generations. Studies completed in the late 1960's, when the bitter conflicts over civil rights and the Indo-China War were assumed to have alienated much of the younger generation from the political system, revealed that most young Americans accepted the same political values and institutional loyalties as their elders although, in many cases, they wanted different policy outputs or some modest institutional reforms.[12] Thus, while regime support is sometimes uneven, and even chronically depressed among the disadvantaged, it is still reasonably strong; certainly there seems to be no major clamor for wholesale constitutional changes.

The lack of sentiment for major constitutional reform, even in times of political stress, underscores one particularly remarkable aspect of American political culture: the "givenness" of the basic governmental system. As historian Daniel Boorstein has remarked, Americans have acted upon "the belief that values in America are in some way or other automatically defined: *given* by certain facts of geography or history peculiar to us." It almost seems, he notes, as if the Founding Fathers "equipped our nation at its birth with a perfect and complete political theory, adequate to all our future needs."[13] It has been necessary to legitimate this political formula by association with the Founding Fathers, the Constitution, and other forms of sanctification as an alternative to tradition, religion, or some other source of legitimacy, but the system has not been challenged for a century. In fact, while Americans often endorse relatively minor constitutional tinkering —altering the electoral college, limiting the term of the President, or lowering the voting age—they show scant interest, let alone enthusiasm, for other forms of government or other political ideologies; parties and leaders committed to such programs have commonly faced bleak prospects and perish unmourned.

In short, regime support may sometimes vacillate across the breadth of the American public but, historically, it has remained stable at relatively high levels among a people who, in any event, demonstrate a minuscule interest in major alternatives.

Political Trust. Americans are vigorously, sometimes feverishly, involved in an enormous variety of group activities. Almost two-thirds of the population belong to some form of organized social group, more than one-third ordinarily spend some leisure time in group activities, and a majority report that a citizen's obligations include a duty to be involved in some civic affairs. Small wonder, then, that Americans have earned a reputation as "a nation of joiners" (of more than 100,000 voluntary associations). Although group activism decreases as one moves down the class hierarchy until it may be very irregular among the most disadvantaged, the vast majority of Americans are both interested and experienced in social collaboration. Underlying this social activity is, apparently, a diffuse trust in others and a confidence in group activity as a salient means for satisfying individual needs. Foreign observers, often viewing Americans more perceptively than Americans see themselves, have long remarked upon the openness to others, optimism, and interest in social affairs that seem part of the American character—a spectrum of traits variously considered refreshing, admirable, or touchingly naive. In any event, this widespread social trust is indicated in Table 3.5, which compares public responses at various points in the last decade to a question involving social attitudes.

In political terms, social trust and a belief in the efficacy of group activity is reflected in the American tradition of forming organized groups for a wide range of temporary or permanent political objectives; *lobbying* is considered a natural form of

TABLE 3.5

Community Trust in the United States and Other
Selected Western Nations, 1960–68.

Question: Some people say that most people can be trusted. Others say
you can't be too careful in your dealings with people. How do you feel
about it?

	United States				*United Kingdom* 1960	*Mexico* 1960
	1968	1966	1964	1960		
Most people can be trusted	55%	52%	53%	55%	49%	30%
You can't be too careful	43	46	45	40	39	65
It depends, other, etc.	2	2	2	5	12	5
N	1,343	1,291	1,450	970	970	970

	West Germany 1960	*Italy* 1969
Most people can be trusted	19%	7%
You can't be too careful	59	83
It depends, other, etc.	22	10
N	970	970

SOURCE: Donald J. Devine, *The Political Culture of the United States*
(Boston: Little, Brown, 1972), p. 100. Slightly adapted.

group political strategy. These groups range from the large trade
and occupational associations through local civic groups mixing
social, charitable, and political objectives (such as the Rotary, or
League of Women Voters) to *ad hoc* organizations formed for
special, transient purposes like raising money for school bonds.
Indeed, so habitual is the American tendency to "form a commit-
tee" on important social concerns—the customary prelude to organization—that almost all groups, even the very unorthodox, feel
compelled to organize to achieve any political purpose. Perhaps
the ultimate tribute to this organizational zeal was the formation
of a lobbying group representing the Hell's Angels' motorcycle
club, a strategy which a club spokesman asserted would give
them a "better image" among public officials.

If social trust is fairly diffuse among Americans, trust in public
officials is more guarded and qualified.[14] Americans have always
been ambivalent toward the political vocation, admiring political

TABLE 3.6

Public Beliefs Concerning Governmental
Responsiveness to Public Opinion

Question: How much attention do you feel the government pays to what the people think when it decides what to do? (SRC)

	1964	1968
Some, or good deal	70%	66%
Not much	24	29
Don't know, no answer	6	5

SOURCE: Donald J. Devine, *The Political Culture of the United States* (Boston: Little, Brown, 1972), p. 148.

heroes and the most prestigious offices such as the Presidency, but simultaneously voicing skepticism about the honesty and efficiency of "politicians." In the middle 1960's, for instance, a fairly typical finding revealed that, although Americans listed the President, state governors, U.S. senators, and Supreme Court justices among the ten most admired occupations in the country, more than half of another sample said they wouldn't like to see their son or daughter go into politics. These inconsistent responses may well mean that Americans rate different political offices differently and that different conceptions of "politics" prevail among the public. Nonetheless, a residual caution, if not strong distrust, is evident among a sizable minority of Americans; this is apparent in Table 3.6, which represents a typical profile of public sentiments through the mid-1960's.

Looking at citizenly trust in comparative terms, it appears that Americans have been somewhat less trustful and less deferential toward their national political leadership than have the British but considerably more active and involved in social action of all kinds. The differences between these two democracies in this respect, however, seem less salient than the evidence that political and social trust in the two nations is considerably higher and more pervasive throughout the society than among most other nations. This social confidence, though sometimes limited, has immensely eased the creation and maintenance of a national government and the establishment of a stable civil order, particularly compared with the experience of many other nations.

Rules of the Game. The official American version of the democratic credo places great weight upon four procedural norms: *equality, freedom, political participation,* and the *rule of law.* During most of its existence, the nation asserted a very outspoken, if not smug, pride in its political freedoms and advertised itself at home and abroad as the world's first and foremost democratic nation. Beginning with early citizenship training, Americans are exposed to constant affirmation of these values until such terms suffuse most political rhetoric and, on ceremonial occasions, become the platitudes of public officials. According to the opinion polls, Americans do express considerable support for these principles and have, with varying success, attempted to implement them throughout their civic affairs. Still, there is a recurring American ambivalence toward these norms—a mixture of acceptance and rejection which shows up in public opinion studies and in the practical conduct of civic affairs. In particular, the widespread discrimination against minorities, especially blacks, who have been denied until recently the protection of these norms, indicates that many Americans are more accepting of these norms in principle than in practice. Even though Americans do affirm most of these norms and seem committed to implementing them (or at least tolerating their implementation), the public is far from unanimously embracing these norms operationally. This ambivalence is revealed in Table 3.7 which displays public responses to a variety of statements concerning political life; the mixed acceptance, rejection, and qualified approval of basic norms revealed in this table would, quite probably, be repeated if the poll were taken today.

In the political sphere, *equality* has been associated with equal protection under the law and other uniform civil rights; in the economic sphere, with equal opportunity for social advancement. The most important political statement of this equality is contained in the constitutional guarantee that civil rights are protected without respect to "race, creed or color." The right to equal economic opportunities, while less clearly stated and implemented, is one of the motive forces behind the establishment of a system of free, compulsory education in the United States. Many civil rights have been ever more widely granted since the

Political Culture

TABLE 3.7
American Beliefs About the "Rules of the Game," 1964

Item	Percentage of Respondents Agreeing with Item
Political Equality	
The majority has the right to abolish minorities if it wants to.	28.4
Sometimes unfairness or brutality may have to be justified when some good purpose is being carried out.	32.8
The laws of this country are supposed to benefit all of us equally, but the fact is that they're almost all "rich man's laws."	33.3
Most people don't have enough sense to pick their own leaders wisely.	47.8
Political Freedom	
Freedom does not give anyone the right to teach foreign ideas in our schools.	56.7
No matter what crime a person is accused of, he should never be convicted unless he has been given the right to face and question his accusers.	88.1
In dealing with dangerous enemies like the Communists, we can't afford to depend on the courts, the laws, and their slow and unreliable methods.	25.5
A man oughtn't to be allowed to speak if he doesn't know what he's talking about.	36.7
Political Participation	
I avoid dealing with public officials as much as I can.	39.3
People ought to be allowed to vote even if they can't do so intelligently.	47.6
Nothing I ever do seems to have any effect upon what happens in politics.	61.5
Rule of Law	
No matter what a person's political beliefs are, he is entitled to the same legal rights and protections as anyone else.	94.3
A poor man doesn't have the chance he deserves in the law courts.	42.9
There are times when it almost seems better for the people to take the law into their own hands rather than wait for the machinery of government to act.	26.9

SOURCE: Herbert McClosky, "Consensus and Ideology in American Politics," *American Political Science Review*, 58 (June, 1964), 361–82.

nation's beginning; and others, such as those which blacks have claimed, have been granted only gradually and after long, arduous struggle. The right to vote, for instance, has been constantly expanded since the Republic's foundation, first to all male whites through the elimination of property requirements (circa 1800), then by the elimination of female exclusion (1919), and, most recently, by extension to young citizens between ages eighteen and twenty-one. Black Americans, particularly in the South, were successful in achieving these rights only in the last decade.

In the United States, *freedom* relates particularly to expressive freedoms, including voting, the rights of petition, peaceable assembly, and publication of political opinions, and to literary expression unsullied by censorship. In these respects, the United States has traditionally been a very open society: governmental and civic activities are generally accompanied by a great deal of noise generated by media commentary and by evaluation from numerous other sources public and private; and, press censorship, while sometimes attempted and occasionally accomplished, has not been a serious problem. In comparative terms, the United States has generally remained a society in which expressive freedoms of all kinds are widely implemented if not always admired. Americans emphasize the importance of several aspects of political participation; they are told, and generally state, that a citizen has a duty to inform himself and to vote in political life, and that the legitimacy of governmental authority is closely tied to the election of major decision-makers. Indeed, Americans have made popular elections almost a fetish and have insisted upon electing 500,000 public officials—more elective officials than any other nation on earth. The importance of legal norms as a guide to civic conduct is reflected in the traditionally high prestige accorded to the judiciary, particularly the Supreme Court, and to the enormous impact it has had upon the conduct of public officials, particularly in the numerous instances where the courts have served to restrain or confound Presidential behavior.

The long history of social discrimination in the United States sufficiently emphasizes how the dominant values of American political culture have been qualified in the past. It is also true that many Americans have difficulty when their principles must be translated into the appropriate practice; they often seem to endorse practical rules for civic conduct that contradict the official norms. This may often be unimportant because the norms will be applied and enforced in practical situations by public officials, especially law enforcement and judicial officials, who must apply the principles with reasonable consistency. Nevertheless, the discrepancy between the public's idealized norms and its preferences in the practical conduct of political life indicates that there may be considerable public tolerance for deviation from the norms. For example, a CBS News poll of 1,136 Americans in mid-1970 indicated:

> About three-fourths of those sampled would not permit extremist groups to demonstrate against the government, even if no clear danger of violence occurred.
>
> About half of those sampled would not give everyone the right to criticize the government if the criticism were thought to damage the national interest.
>
> Nearly three-fifths of those sampled believed that if a person was found innocent of a serious crime but new evidence was uncovered after the trial he should be tried again.
>
> About three-fifths of those sampled believed the police should hold a man in jail if they suspected him of a serious crime until they can find enough evidence to charge him.[15]

If taken at face value, this poll suggests that a majority of Americans would be willing to limit free speech seriously, to submit a man to double jeopardy, and to suspend the writ of *habeas corpus*, all clearly contradicting the Bill of Rights. Many Americans might not be willing to accept such a conclusion when baldly stated, but it does seem apparent that many, at least in the abstract, are willing to contemplate political norms quite at variance with the official norms; such evidence casts considerable doubt upon any notions of a "great consensus" on fundamental political rules of the game among Americans.

Political Competence and Efficacy. Americans customarily express a conviction that they can influence the conduct of government—most polls report that almost two-thirds of respondents believe they have some say in what government does—and most

TABLE 3.8
Percentages of Americans Professing to Having Been
Active in Various Political Activities, 1952–70

Activity	1952	1956	1960	1964	1968	1970
Belong to political club	2	3	3	4	3	5
Work for political party	3	3	6	5	5	7
Attend political rally or meeting	7	10	8	9	9	9
Contribute money to campaign	4	10	12	11	9	a
Use political sticker or button	–	16	21	16	15	9
Give political opinions	27	28	33	31	30	27
Vote in election	73	73	74	78	75	59

a Not asked.

SOURCE: Robert S. Erikson and Normal R. Luttbeg, *American Public Opinion* (New York: John Wiley and Sons, 1973), p. 5.

assert that civic activism is the obligation of a good citizen. In reality, however, the average American is relatively passive politically. An estimate of civic activism among Americans can be found in Table 3.8, which indicates the proportion of citizens reporting various political activities between 1952 and 1970.

As this Table implies, most Americans end their civic activism with voting; the political life of the nation is largely conducted by a handful of individuals. According to one estimate, about one-fifth of Americans engaged in another of these activities beyond voting, only 8 per cent engaged in two additional activities, and only 7 per cent in three or more.[16] There are several likely explanations for this low civic involvement. Politics is not sufficiently important or interesting to engage the attention of Americans most of the time; public opinion studies usually indicate that most people are mainly preoccupied with personal concerns and family matters (one estimate suggests that three-quarters of the population spends most of its time worrying about economic and personal matters while only about one-fifth spend considerable time with matters political). Moreover, Americans tend to regard voting as the most effective way of influencing government.[17] The majority of Americans, additionally, seem to find political affairs a baffling business much of the time; expressions of confusion and discouragement from efforts to make sense of political life are common in opinion studies. Low levels of political activism and some frustration over efforts to interpret political affairs do not necessarily imply political alienation or cynicism; indeed, many commentators have suggested that low levels of political interest and activism, in cases where greater involvement is largely at the discretion of the citizen, may imply a high level of residual contentment and trust toward both public officials and the conduct of civic affairs—in effect, most citizens may be content to neglect civic affairs because they feel no crisis or threat arising from the political system.

Despite these vagaries of the American public's attitude toward politics and activism, Americans have been, in comparative terms, a people with a generally high level of political competence, and political activity, while often limited, is still more frequent than in most other major political systems about which survey data is available. In short, Americans may not fulfill their own idealized image of the "ideal citizen," but they do maintain a vigorous civic life and, when they feel it necessary, seem capable of political involvement in many forms.

The severest test of accomplishment for any nation is to judge it by the standard of its idealized political norms; all polities will fail in some degree to satisfy the measure. Neither the United States nor Great Britain can claim to have approached the ideal democratic political order although, in comparative terms, both seem to have come closer than most other countries. In a similar vein, neither nation approaches a pure *integrated* political culture as scholars have defined integration at the theoretical level. Nonetheless, the extent to which the political cultures of both nations have been integrated is still impressive, particularly when they are compared to the fragmented political cultures. This cultural integration can be appreciated best if we turn, in the next chapter, to examining two fragmented political systems in some detail.

NOTES

1. The political implications of English history are summarized in Richard Rose, *England* (Boston: Little, Brown, 1964), chapters 1 and 2.

2. Age has only improved Bagehot's insight into British character. See Walter Bagehot, *The English Constitution* (London: World's Classics Edition, 1955).

3. Gabriel Almond and Sidney Verba, *The Civic Culture* (Boston: Little, Brown, 1965), p. 99.

4. Bagehot, *op. cit.*, p. 141.

5. Rose, *op. cit.*, p. 41.

6. David Butler and Donald Stokes, *Political Change in Britain* (New York: St. Martin's Press, 1969), p. 25.

7. *Ibid.*, pp. 32–33.

8. Almond and Verba, *op. cit.*, p. 54.

9. Jack Dennis, Leon Lindberg, and Donald McCrone, "Support for Nation and Government Among English School Children," *British Journal of Political Science*, I, Part I (January, 1971), p. 33.

10. A stimulating interpretation of American history in the context of political development is Seymour M. Lipset, *The First New Nation* (New York: Basic Books, 1963).

11. The continuing existence of regime distrust among blacks is documented in two recent studies: Joel D. Aberbach and Jack L. Walker, *Race in the City* (Boston: Little, Brown, 1973), esp. chapter 6; and David O. Sears and John B. McConahay, *The Politics of Violence* (Boston: Houghton, Mifflin, 1973).

12. See Donald J. Devine, *The Political Culture of the United States* (Boston: Little, Brown, 1972), pp. 273–74.

13. Daniel J. Boorstein, *The Genius of American Politics* (Chicago: University of Chicago Press, 1953), p. 9.

14. The vacillations in public trust of officials is recorded by the Center for Political Studies, Survey Research Center, University of Michigan, and regularly reported in the Center's *Bulletin.*

15. Reported by James Reston in *The New York Times*, April 19, 1970.

16. John P. Robinson, Jerrold G. Rusk, and Kendra Head, *Measures of Political Attitudes* (Survey Research Center, Institute of Social Research, U. of Michigan, 1968), pp. 594–96.

17. In addition to materials available on voting through the University of Michigan's Center for Political Studies, see Lester W. Milbrath, *Political Participation* (Chicago: Rand McNally, 1965), chapter vi.

4

TWO STUDIES IN POLITICAL FRAGMENTATION: ITALY AND ZAIRE

Italy has been described as a nation of the politically cynical and alienated, where the cultural elements "maintain at best an armed truce and, at worst, open hostility"; most citizens do not even think of themselves as subjects in the sense of "accepting as legitimate or justifiable the institutions and the outputs of the political system."[1] The Congo has been nominated as "a candidate for Africa's leading laboratory of violence," where civil strife has so disrupted the political process that no national government existed for long periods. Italy and the Congo represent two variations upon the common theme of political culture fragmentation. While this political fragmentation assumes very different forms in the two countries, underlying these disparate manifestations of civic disorder are a number of sources common to fragmented cultures generally.

Italy's fragmentation seems the less virulent. Political disaffection and social antagonism, though occasionally erupting into violence, most often produce a greatly diminished governmental effectiveness, a chronic inability of national government to mobilize the human and material resources needed to meet the nation's major social ills. Collaboration among major social groups is ordinarily difficult, often impossible, so that internal democracy has been difficult. In contrast, the Congo has repeatedly endured vicious civil wars emanating from tribal, religious, and regional cleavages; the dominant political issue has often been whether there would be any national government at all. In the absence of a stable national government and a sense of national community, the Congo has had to struggle to maintain the rudiments of a nation-state.

The geneses of these disorders are problems we have come to associate with fragmented political cultures. There is a widespread lack of public trust and identification with national government, often emanating from a tenuous belief in the legitimacy of the national political system. Historically deep antagonisms separate social groups clinging to parochial identification with family, region, class, or ethnic group above all competing claims of national government. This parochialism and social suspicion inhibit a sense of political community and political collaboration; group conflicts commonly threaten one side or another deeply, and violence is always a possible result. Not surprisingly, in such a climate national governments have often been impotent or ineffectual. Group conflict often admits of no compromise; national leaders do not feel sufficient political support to attempt difficult policies, however necessary; governmental planning is often conservative and timid. Governmental resources may be very limited because they cannot penetrate the society to mobilize the human and material resources for more ambitious programs. This does not necessarily mean the collapse of the national state or complete governmental immobilism, but it means a constant state of governmental ineffectiveness and citizen political alienation which breeds further disorders.

ITALY

Italian political culture is riddled with jarring, contradictory orientations and deep social cleavages. It is routinely described in terms of unreconciled tensions, of a civic mood permeated with "alienation," "suspicion," and "disaffection"; analysts so often dwell upon the incompetence of government and the political contempt of the masses that one might well wonder why the Italian state exists at all. In fact, Italy has existed as a national state for more than a century, during which it has grown from a predominantly rural nation into a leading industrial nation. Although many of its 52 million people are poor and the land is crowded,

Italy's material culture and standard of living are comparable to other Western European nations.[2] Further, Italy has maintained essentially its present national borders and has supported a national government functioning during all this time despite a disastrous involvement in two world wars; there are no serious separatist movements on the Italian peninsula and political violence, though sometimes massive, is not chronic. The Italians, in brief, have managed to create and even to advance the development of a modern state in many respects.

A paradox of Italian politics is that the Italians have managed to develop many of the political and economic forms of a modern nation while still preserving a political culture that seems hostile to a strong national political order. This "lag" between economic and governmental development, on one side, and the underlying political culture, on the other, is the most important in a series of discontinuities that run through Italian society and account for much of its political fragmentation. Another contrast lies in the difference between the heavily industrialized, urban North—including one of the major industrial complexes of Europe in the Northwestern Triangle of cities (Turin, Milan, and Genoa)—and the South, whose primarily agricultural population maintains the small family farms, sharecropping system, village culture, and other life styles reminiscent of an earlier era. Half the nation's farm population has deserted the land since 1954 but Italy, with one-fifth of its people engaged in agriculture, still has the largest rural population in Western Europe. In good measure, these different regional economies represent antagonistic cultures. The North, dominated by German and Celtic influences, is modern in life style, comparatively affluent, and increasingly secular in outlook; the South, whose antecedents are Greek, Spanish, and Byzantine, is more socially and politically conservative, more attached to the Church, and considerably poorer. Out of such diversity have grown enduring conflicts:

> North and South are hostile to each other, and this fact contributes considerably to the country's lack of political consensus and integration. The Northerner describes his countrymen to the South as indolent and shiftless, *furbo*, or crafty in their human relationships,

illiterate or at least ignorant and therefore incapable of developing or managing modern economic or commercial enterprises, politically corrupt and prone to use public administration as a dumping ground for sons who are incapable of doing anything else.[3]

Yet another contrast lies in religion. Italy is overwhelmingly Catholic (more than 99 per cent of the population formally belong to the Church) and, as the state religion, Catholicism is taught in all public schools. Nonetheless, a strong anticlericalism runs through Italian social and political life. In political affairs, this cleavage is most manifest in the conflict between the Christian Democrats, the nation's largest political party and partisan arm of the Vatican, and the parties of the Left, especially the Socialists and Communists, who together represent more than one-third of the electorate. The Church has been very ambivalent toward the Italian state. The Vatican bitterly opposed Italy's unification in 1870 and refused to recognize the resulting republic fully until 1929; it forbade Catholics to vote until 1904. This implacable hostility, particularly influential with the peasantry, caused the state to retaliate with strong anticlerical measures modified only after a formal reconciliation, the *Concordat*, was signed in 1929. The signing of the Concordat did not eliminate the tension between church and state. The Vatican frequently reasserts that its involvement in secular politics is largely an effort to redeem the nation's morally degenerate government and leaders from their spiritual debasement. The Vatican has repeatedly asserted its right to instruct, and if necessary to order, its congregation regarding political behavior. According to a 1960 statement, for instance, the Church declared that the political conduct of all its members must correspond to church teaching, that priests may dictate the conditions under which Catholics may participate with agnostics in politics, that Catholics must not collaborate with Socialists or Communists, and that every Catholic (including public officials) must follow the Vatican teachings in civic affairs—this last *dictum* posing quite a dilemma for the nation's political leaders sworn to defend the constitution.[4] The Church, notes one scholar, continues to be deeply involved in politics "in every conceivable way short of

electing priests and nuns to legislative and executive bodies,"
with the result that the nation is dichotomized between the faith-
ful and those "who see such involvement as threats to democratic
institutions or at least to their own interests."[5]

Still another divisive element is the conflict between the major classes in Italy's rather rigidly stratified social system. Italian
history is a chronicle of political contention often verging on class
war between the lower class and the middle class, which sets the
style and objectives of national government. Traditionally, the
nation's political leadership is recruited from the middle class.
This has been quite often a reactionary class, stoutly resisting
worker and peasant demands for a greater voice in national politics—such as the right to vote—and overriding the opposition of
lower-class parties and spokesmen until forced to yield grudging
concessions. Workers and peasants have blamed the middle class
for Italy's military calamities in the two world wars. The Fascist
regime that controlled the nation between 1922 and 1945 largely
rose to power on a wave of middle-class resentment against the
growing political influence of workers and peasants. The lower
classes still regard Benito Mussolini as a middle-class scourge un-
loosed upon them in retaliation for their political aggressiveness.
Considerable discrimination against workers and peasants still
exists with the tacit approval of middle-class politicians; in an
educational system where only three of every hundred children
entering public school will finish college, a son or daughter of the
worker or peasant rarely joins this educational elite. In a nation
where class distinctions have been emphasized by contrasting
speech, attire, titles, and other badges of social identity, the intensification of class consciousness by political cleavages has further inhibited social trust. Intellectuals form yet another social
group, alienated from the middle or lower classes; intellectuals
commonly hold almost all other social groups (and the government surely) in contempt, many asserting that Italians have got-
ten precisely the government they deserve.

It may be that these social cleavages are slowly softening with
growing industrialization, social mobility, the emerging national
pride in the country's economic miracle, and other influences
emerging since World War II. Yet these conflicts run deep and

broad through Italian history and still set the dominant tone of the political culture in many critical respects.

Regime Orientations. In their study of political culture, Almond and Verba discovered that only 4 per cent of their Italian respondents expressed any spontaneous pride in their national government—the lowest figure in this category among all the nations studied. "Italians in the overwhelming majority take no pride in their political system, nor even in their economy or society," remarked the researchers. "To the extent that they have national pride at all, it is in their history, the physical beauty of their country, or in the fact of being Italian."[6] Not all the data collected in this or later studies reveals unrelieved political alienation—for example, a majority of Italians in the Almond and Verba work felt they would receive fair and equal treatment from their own police and administrative bureaucracies, and later studies of Italian school children suggest that they, at least, are confident of having influence and importance in political affairs. Still, alienation is widespread and persistent in Italian culture and seems to be more pervasive than in any other Western European country.

This political alienation is rooted in Italian history. Italy was united "from above," through the military force applied to the various Italian states by the Kingdom of Sardinia. A national plebiscite in 1870 formally ratified the new Republic of Italy, but the election was fraudulently conducted in many areas, particularly in the South. Shortly after this coercive unification, a central government and administration supplanted most local governmental institutions and customs. The Italian masses took little part in the process of nation building, felt little identification with a frequently remote national government and its political symbols, and were further alienated by the rapid abolition of local political institutions and practices. Thus, the Italian state developed without an antecedent sense of political community or the national myths which rally public allegiance to the common symbols and institutions supposed to represent the new state. Time did little to foster a broader consensus. Following the Allied invasion and defeat of Italy during World War II, a national plebiscite was held on the form of a new constitution; the existing constitution won a bare majority, but 45 per cent of the voters, including a majority in the South, preferred the former monarchy to the present republic. Since 1945, the miracle of Italy's burgeoning economy has done much to develop a sense of pride in the country, and the social transformations produced by industrialization have increased the sense of common nationality among Italians. But there does not seem to be a growing mass confidence in, or identification with, national political institutions, particularly in the South, where the majority of Italian peasants live and parochial loyalties are still intense.

The cynical Italian's low esteem of the governmental system may be justified. The parliamentary leadership, often irresolute in the face of major problems, is usually content to drift; the national administrative structure with which most Italians have constant contact is often inefficient, conservative, and corrupt; politicians and bureaucrats often seem petty and venal. According to many Italians, an intelligent citizen will not go to court unless he knows he is wrong; if he is right, he is likely to be cheated of his just reward, but if he is wrong, the delay and ineptitude of the judges will probably save him at the expense of his adversary. The income tax is administered with a genius for alienating the average citizen.

> . . . since the government assumes that most taxpayers are chronic liars, many tax returns are almost automatically scaled upward by the tax authorities. Anyone who turns in an honest report of his true income . . . is apt to have his assessment arbitrarily raised. The final decision concerning the actual tax may frequently be the result of a lengthy process of negotiation. At the local level, assessment of liability for the family tax provides the party (or parties) in power with an opportunity to reward their friends and punish their enemies: Businessmen who fail to contribute funds to the party or who support minority parties may have to shoulder an unusually heavy tax burden.[7]

Governmental corruption has moved the Vatican to advise priests hearing confessions that it is not a sin for a citizen to bribe a public servant when it is the only way a citizen can get a service for which he has a right and it is not necessarily a transgression for public officials to accept the favor. Public services are often pro-

vided with bland arrogance. The electric company considers it
proper to end services to a customer without any warning if the
customer has failed to pay a bill he has not received; "the tele-
phone company requires full payment of whatever sum for which
it cares to consider a subscriber liable before it will even consent
to inform him of the destination of a long distance call for which
he is being charged."[8]

Such constant governmental chicanery is bound to undermine
public confidence and cooperativeness toward the regime, and
explains the widespread civic contempt for regime norms and institutions; for most Italians, the regime remains a grinding, predatory mechanism.

Political Trust. Many studies strongly suggest that the average
Italian distrusts not only his government but also his neighbor,
that his affections seldom extend beyond family, village, region,
or peer group. This may be exaggerated, for we shall see later
that Italians frequently participate in political and civic affairs,
though less frequently than the British or Americans; there is,
however, a more pervasive suspicion in Italian social life than in
most other European nations. This frequently appears as a conviction that others might use personal revelations against one,
that one probably does not share many values with different social groups and—particularly important to political affairs—that
political information about an individual might be used as a
weapon to injure him through the political process. Thus, Almond and Verba found that two-thirds of their Italian respondents reported *never* talking to others about politics, and one-third
refused to tell the interviewers how they voted in national elections—much larger fractions than in any of the other nations under study. In partisan affairs, writes Joseph LaPolombara, "the
typical Italian feels that elections are contests among mutually
and fundamentally antagonistic groups—between the 'we' and
'the enemy.' It is assumed that the winners will take advantage
of and exploit the losers."[9] Even the industrialist at the top of the
social ladder is likely to be slightly paranoid toward his social
milieu, seeing himself "involved in vicious class warfare from
which there is no escape and in which the posture of the industrial group remains largely defensive."[10]

This social suspicion, once inherited, is perpetuated by the tendency of social groups to form mutually exclusive social and political associations without the overlapping memberships and experiences in social collaboration that breed more tolerance. Thus, there are workers' unions organized for Catholics, Socialists, Communists, students, and even Fascists; the same will be true of athletic clubs, recreational associations, intellectual and literary groups, and almost all other voluntary associations. Within these groups the members are likely to be indoctrinated into a belief that the government is corrupt, the bureaucracy incompetent, the political parties untrustworthy. The ultimate political expression of this social distrust is the Italian party system, which is fragmented into Socialist, Communist, Catholic, Conservative, and Fascist parties drawing their membership from distinctly different social groupings.

Many observers trace this social suspicion to the socialization of children in the Italian family. It is often asserted that Italian children are taught early to distrust others, particularly those outside the family and peer group, and to look out for self and family above all. This pattern of socialization is frequently associated with the peasant and worker culture which traditionally incorporates the majority of Italians. While some commentators assert that this numerical distribution may be changing with industrialization, social mobility, and the slow breakdown of village life, particularly in the South, social suspicion continues to be an important theme in Italian social affairs.

Rules of the Game. The norms which most Italians appear to accept as guidelines for their political behavior and their subjective beliefs about political conduct grow from, and further intensify, the atmosphere of alienation and suspicion in Italian politics.

The political elite, almost completely middle class, practices a highly ideological, abstract, and rigid style of political discussion, which inhibits political compromise and bores most other Italians. Much of this rigidity is undoubtedly due to historic social cleavages and the resulting suspiciousness, but many observers trace the lack of compromise and bargaining among the political leadership to the Italian educational system, which fails to equip the nation's elite for thinking about social problems pragmatically and empirically. In a political system where party programs are elevated to the level of moral principles and bound into a tight philosophical structure, it is quite difficult for leaders to compromise or modify programs without internal criticism from their own party organizations; one result is that Italian political parties have a frequent tendency to splinter into new ideological factions. At the same time, middle-class political leaders generally assume that it is proper and necessary for them to hold the reins of government and for their social constituency to dominate Italian politics.

The mass of Italians appear to have a "subject orientation" in their assumption about appropriate political behavior. They place no great emphasis upon civic participation or knowledge; they often see themselves affected by government but seldom influencing it. In a great many respects, they believe government is run by "them" (as opposed to "we"), and common attitudes seem to imply that a man's responsibility is to protect himself from a predatory government and to beat the politicians and bureaucrats at their own crooked game. Certainly, most Italians express scant interest in political discussion; many feel it is dangerous to admit political viewpoints or voting preferences to others—Almond and Verba found that 34 per cent of their respondents felt free to discuss politics with no one, and another 17 per cent confined discussion to a very selective group.[11] Partisans of one party quite commonly express strong hostility to those of another and, consequently, political discussions often end quite unpleasantly. Given the disagreeable overtones so often found in political life, the average Italian frequently attempts to anesthetize himself against political affairs whenever possible. Although such attitudes are seldom found among the better educated Italians, who more often stress the importance of political participation, of their competence in civic life, and of allegiant sentiments toward national government, these sentiments still represent a minority of the population.[12]

In a political system where the majority so often find the leadership style irrelevant or incomprehensible and where a strong presumption of governmental malice ordinarily exists, political violence may have a particular appeal as a protest weapon. Italian politics has a long tradition of violence—street riots, assaults on public buildings, confrontations between police and demonstrators—which many experts view as an important device for getting the attention of the population. This is "controlled catharsis" in the sense that violence is seldom carried to the point where killings or wholesale destruction results, but it is often used as a strategy by political leaders within a culture which accepts its controlled use as necessary, if not legitimate. Short of violence, protest against government is most often expressed by voting for opposition parties committed to radical reconstruction of the Italian Constitution, or to its abolition. The Italian Communist Party, the largest Marxist party in Europe with more than one-quarter of the Italian popular vote, has been the most common outlet for the protest vote; when the other Marxist parties (mostly socialist) are considered in addition to the Communists, more than 45 per cent of the Italian electorate has voted for parties opposed to most of the major regime policies and structures. In recent years, many commentators have come to believe that the Communist Party does not represent a truly Marxist revolutionary outlook and may, if it assumes power, accept the basic features of the Constitution; even so, the near majority of Italians recently voting for parties strongly opposed to the current regime still bespeaks the intensity of disaffection with government found among the Italian masses.

Another rule of the game widely practiced among Italians is the resort to legalism for setting social problems. Italians tend to turn, almost habitually, to the judicial process as the method for resolving a major controversy, using the law and its rigid application as a surrogate for accommodation and the informal settlement of social disagreements. This reliance upon the judiciary has often resulted in a highly artificial and abstract legal logic being applied to social and political controversies, because Italian jurists, like politicians, have little training in the more pragmatic, empirical, and common-law approach to litigation found in the United States or Great Britain. In the absence of widespread social amiability and political trust, resort to the legal process has often seemed the only recourse short of violence available to Italians trying to preserve a semblance of order and civility in the political process.

Political Competence and Efficacy. In a nation suffused with political cynicism, it seems surprising that Italians vote and affiliate with political parties in far greater proportions than citizens in most other democracies. But the average Italian apparently votes without a conviction that his ballot will affect the course of government, carries his party card without participating in much party activity, and believes that his civic obligations are not extensive or important. Thus, voting and party membership become a ritual, a rather sterile activity uninspired by a genuine or widespread sense of civic competence.

Italy customarily leads the democratic nations in the proportions of its electorate appearing at the polls—usually in excess of 90 per cent; many commentators attribute this high turnout less to strong public interest in elections than to the nation's compulsory voting requirements and convenient arrangements for polling. Italy's political parties are among the world's largest: the Communists (1.7 million members), Christian Democrats (1.6 million) and Socialists (0.6 million) lead the multitude of other parties which, all together, enroll approximately 12 per cent of the Italian electorate. But only a tiny proportion of Italians participate in party activities (although many may belong to party-affiliated interest groups) and membership is often attributed to the habit of party registration developed during the Fascist period.

In any event, whatever civic rituals the Italians practice does not seem to have inspired a strong sense of political competence or efficacy among the population. According to survey research, only 5 per cent believe that a citizen has an obligation to participate in civic life.[13] Italians generally express some confidence in their ability to participate effectively in local government, but less than one-third of the population apparently believes it can do anything about an unjust national law. After carefully surveying public sentiments concerning political competence, Almond and Verba concluded that only about 27 per cent of the Italian population could be considered to believe that they could effectively influence government at both local and national levels—the lowest proportion of individuals expressing this belief among the five nations studied. So widespread is political disinterest that a large proportion of Italians are reported to feel neither enjoy-

ment, anger, nor contempt toward campaigns, perhaps the ultimate stage of civic stupor.

It is also true that Italians have not been exposed in the past to
the stimulation to political participation and interest provided by
the mass media. Italian newspapers, for example, are notoriously
dull on matters political, preferring to discuss politics at a forbid-
dingly abstract level; until recently, the state-controlled television
network did not offer a generous variety of political viewpoints
or debates for public consumption, and many Italians are likely,
in any event, to presume the news is being manipulated solely to
the advantage of the reigning political parties. In the South,
where parochial loyalties and interests still dominate, the media
are prone to cater to the social preoccupations of the public
rather than to elevate its level of political information or interest.

Thus, high rates of participation in party activity and elections
prove to be little more than gloss covering a political culture
largely devoid of citizens with a strong interest in politics or confidence in their political effectiveness, a culture of the politically
apathetic and disenchanted.

A Faint Stirring of Optimism. The most effective countervailing influence against the fragmentary forces in Italian political
life may prove to be urbanization and its associated social ramifications, which may slowly erode the social animosities now so
prominent. In particular, the steady immigration from the farms
to the city and from the South to the North may eventually eradi-
cate the divisive influence on Italian politics of parochial loyalties
and rural outlooks. Growing urbanization may bring a more
evenly dispersed affluence and the increased social mobility
that inhibits social antagonisms. If urbanization continues at its
present pace in Italy, the result is likely to be a much more socially homogeneous population, one more secular and less tied to
traditional modes of political thinking and action. At the same
time, social cleavages have been historic and deep; it is far too
early to predict that even the powerful transforming influence of
urbanization and affluence will be sufficient to blunt the fragmentary currents so long dominating Italian social life.

THE CONGO (ZAIRE)

The Democratic Republic of the Congo (now the Republic of Zaire) began in 1885 as the Belgian Free State, annexed by King Leopold II as his personal property until the Belgian Parliament and people could be persuaded to incorporate it within the nation as a colony. In 1908 Belgium finally absorbed the Free State, renamed it the Belgian Congo, and remained its colonial overlord until 1960 when the colony formally declared independence and called itself the Democratic Republic of the Congo. The republic, one of Africa's largest nations, is rather sparsely populated by 17 million natives, divided among more than 200 tribal groups, and perhaps 150,000 Europeans, primarily Belgian expatriates. Although 3 million of its people live within urban areas, mostly around Kinshasa (formerly Leopoldville), Kisangani (Stanleyville), and Lubumbashi (Elizabethville), more than two of every three Congolese still live in rural settlements or small towns. The modern Congolese economy, flourishing upon an economic base earlier provided by rubber and ivory exportation, is now extremely productive in the mining of tin and copper (particularly in the old Katanga Province), diamonds, and gold.

The Democratic Republic of the Congo was born in a political bloodbath on a scale unwitnessed in any other emerging African state since World War II. The chronic political crises and civil violence of its earliest years were magnified by the news media until the Congo became synonymous with political disorder verging upon anarchy. In recent years a measure of internal order and governmental continuity has been achieved; nevertheless, the Congo remains a singular example of the most malevolent aspect of political culture fragmentation. The sources of this fragmentation are complex, some found in the process of "decolonization" common to many African states, some inherent in fragmented political cultures, and some unique to the Congo. Interpreting Congolese political culture is further complicated by the lack of survey data often accumulated over long time periods in other polities. Still, the salient aspects of Congolese political culture can be inferred from many studies and described in broad outline. As a preliminary, it is useful to survey briefly the nation's early political history to illuminate the gravity of the political fragmentation.

A Cycle of Crises. The extreme fragmentation of Congolese political culture appeared almost from the moment of its independence. During the first years of national existence, this fragmentation expressed itself largely as a mosaic of violence, erupting early and spreading rapidly, then subsiding into a tenuous peace only to renew itself in a display of savagery concluded by the abandonment of the original constitutional system.[14]

The first wave of political disorder, beginning almost immediately after national independence in June, 1960, extended until mid-1963. Within its first six months of independence, the country had disintegrated into three secessionist provinces (Sud-Kasai, Katanga, and Stanleyville) each claiming independence from the central government in Leopoldville; native troops of the Armée Nationale Congolaise, having mutinied against their European and native officers less than a month after independence, had splintered into belligerent factions which were drawn by tribal and ethnic loyalties to one or another of the secessionist fragments until each territorial unit had its own militia. At the political level, the first Prime Minister, Patrice Lumumba, was dismissed by the President of the Republic, captured in his flight to the rival "national government" established by his supporters in Stanleyville, and assassinated by army units loyal to the central government. The central government itself was temporarily seized by army units loyal to Colonel Joseph Mobutu; the President of the Republic, Joseph Kasavubu, facing provincial secession and possessing an impotent remnant of the national army incapable of restoring order, appealed to the United Nations for military assistance in bringing Katanga back to the confederation. United Nations forces responded by entering the Congo and initiating a series of campaigns against the secessionist forces loyal to the Katanga regime. During this period, national government was largely a pretense. "From July 1 to September 29, 1961," wrote one government official, "the country was no longer really governed. No law, no ordinance, no important decision was made. . . . Within the administration, the functionaries, lacking top echelon personnel and governmental directives, found it impossible to make the administrative machine function."[15]

During 1961 and 1962 a measure of order was restored. A new civilian government and Prime Minister emerged in Leopoldville. With the aid of U.N. forces, the government gradually forced Katanga Province back into the confederation and subdued dissidents in the other breakaway areas; by September, 1963, the central government felt sufficiently strong to order a commission to draft a new constitution for the country. Nevertheless, the country was never free from violence, particularly in the countryside. Marauding guerilla bands, freebooting segments of the former Armée Nationale Congolaise, imported white mercenaries, and roving bands of youths engaged in intermittent battles in the name of different political factions or self-proclaimed factional leaders. Indiscriminate violence was particularly deadly against luckless Europeans and natives encountering these armed groups. At least fifty prominent political leaders were assassinated and perhaps thousands of civilians died.

In mid-1964 the fragile peace maintained during most of 1963 collapsed, and a second wave of violence began. The economy had become sluggish; central government services, erratic at best, were often moribund, and provincial authorities seldom exercised influence beyond provincial capitals. In July, 1964, a new Prime Minister formed a government and invited the United States and Belgium to provide military assistance in quelling a renewed revolt in Katanga; white mercenaries were also brought to the aid of the Armée Congolaise in combatting this and other internal insurrections. The violence assumed an unparalleled viciousness for a postcolonial nation. One aspect was the march of a "People's Army" to seize control of the Stanleyville Government in August, 1964. This ragtag "army" consisted mostly of rural Congolese youths inflamed by ethnic and economic grievances to take vengeance on real and imagined enemies including older civil servants, families of persons collaborating with the national government, captured national army members, and those accused of being "Americanized." A second major insurrection began in Kwilu Province where guerilla bands, inspired by charismatic leaders, roamed the province, killing local political and administrative officers, teachers, soldiers, and other "reactionaries"; these bands, armed commonly with spears and machetes, easily routed the Congolese Army contingents sent against them until native troops were fortified by white mercenaries and disciplined by European and American advisers. While this terror was sometimes justified by the leaders in vaguely ideological, political, or religious terms, much of the motivation sprang from tribal and ethnic grudges, economic jealousies, and a host of random grievances deeply embedded in rural cultures. Before the central government suppressed these insurrections, at least twenty thousand Congolese and hundreds of Europeans had been murdered, often with extreme brutality.

The turmoil was drastically reduced when Colonel Joseph Mobutu seized the central government in mid-1965 proclaiming himself President. The accession to power of a military strong man gradually brought a restoration of central governmental services, a tightening of discipline in the administrative structure, and a more dependable civil order; diplomacy was again possible abroad and a measure of economic prosperity, born of civil order, returned. At the same time, political violence was transformed from mass disorder to institutionalized attacks upon political opponents of the regime. In May, 1966, Mobutu, charging that an army plot had developed to overturn his government, publicly executed former Prime Minister Evariste Kimba and other government officials; in March, 1967, former Prime Minister Moise Tshombe was condemned to death in exile for alleged plots against the central government. While scattered episodes of violence occurred, they were only faintly reminiscent of the earlier bloodshed. Thus, beginning in 1966, the Congo achieved for the first time a measure of civil order and governmental continuity, which it continues to enjoy under the tutelage of the military government. The constitution of 1967—the third since the Congo's independence—largely strengthened the hand of the President at the expense of both the Parliament and opposition elements.

It is easy to perceive within the Congolese polity many of the characteristics common to fragmented political cultures: the dominance of parochial loyalties over national ones, the lack of consensus upon political rules and political obligations, the absence of political trust, widespread lack of identification with the national government and its symbols, and much else. For one concerned with political culture, the more important issues are how this fragmentation occurred, how it manifested itself and—perhaps most intriguing—why the architects of national independence deluded themselves into believing they had a viable cultural foundation for national government when, in retrospect, the facts seem so utterly contradictory. To answer these questions, one must begin with the crucial year immediately preceding the declaration of Congolese independence and must examine in particular the *decolonization* phase which led to independence.

Government Without Consensus. The Democratic Republic of the Congo began its independence lacking either mass or elite consensus about the nature of the political system, and with a population inexperienced in the political skills requisite for managing the political structures ordained by the first Congolese constitution, the *Loi Fondamentale.* An absence of the cultural underpinnings appropriate to a national government is attributable to the nature of the Congolese colonial experience and to the extraordinary haste with which the Congolese were catapulted from colonial subjugation to national independence. Nowhere in Africa did decolonization occur with less preparation.

Congolese political fragmentation originated in the Belgian colonial philosophy. The Belgian Government, steadfastly refusing to contemplate the termination of its colonial empire until the last moment, gave virtually no attention to nurturing native political institutions, skills, and outlooks appropriate to self-government. Rather, Belgian policy was extremely paternalistic, emphasizing the economic and social development of the population (in terms acceptable to the colonizer) at the expense of native political education. As late as five years prior to independence, no major political parties or self-governing native institutions of consequence existed in the Congo. The administrative arm of the Belgian colonial regime, penetrating Congolese society with a thoroughness and persuasiveness unmatched in any other colonial system, had oriented the Congolese to a largely passive, acquiescent, and "subject" posture toward government: policy came from above, without extensive native consultation, and without much evidence that native sentiments were widely considered or effective in decision-making. The average Congolese had little experience in personal independence, let alone political autonomy or responsibility. Few Congolese could own property, nightly curfews were enforced, and only after 1955 could liquor be purchased legally. Native education, accomplished primarily through the extensive Catholic missionary schools collaborating with the state, inculcated skills necessary for work in the major economic enterprises of the country and socialized youngsters into their colonial political role. In the mid-1950's, less than a decade from national independence, the average Congolese had received a rudimentary education terminating, at best, with secondary schooling; he was reasonably well cared for medically, had adequate shelter and, in most cases, an adequate living (measured in terms of the average level of economic accomplishment in the nation), and was very slowly acquiring some of the skills and outlooks characteristic of a worker in modern industry. But in terms of civic outlook, he was, with few exceptions, a pure subject.

Had there been time enough and will, the Congolese—or at least the national elite—might have been educated into political orientations compatible with national independence. But decolonization overtook both rulers and ruled with a speed for which neither was prepared. In 1955 the previously productive Congolese economy fell into recession, confronting the Belgian Government with the prospect of heavy colonial subsidies, and forcing it to examine critically the ongoing value of its African territory at a time when its parliamentary parties had begun to debate the merits of continued colonization. The first faint stirrings of nationalism were moving the Congolese elite to press, gently at first but with increasing urgency, for Belgian declaration of the terminal date for colonial rule. As late as 1957, however, the Belgian Government, still thinking in terms of decades instead of months until independence, assumed it would control the pace of decolonization and assist a cooperative Congolese elite leading a subdued mass to gradual emancipation. Believing that militant nationalism would not agitate the Congolese masses or elite, Belgium assumed that there was generous time available in which to create the political skills, structures, and formulas upon which Congolese independence could be securely erected. However, the Belgian Government badly misperceived the intensity of native hunger for independence and the brittleness of its own authority in the Congo. In January, 1959, widespread riots in Leopoldville shocked the Belgian leadership into recognizing the true strength of Congolese nationalism and convinced it to promise an almost immediate end to a colonial system in which it had largely lost faith itself.

Suddenly, with Congolese independence almost upon it, the Belgian Government had to collaborate with the native elite in constructing the whole scaffolding of provincial and national government within four months; this, notes one commentator, amounted to "virtually improvising from scratch a political system," including all the trappings of "democracy" until then largely unfamiliar to the native population.[16] What emerged from these deliberations was initially accepted by both Belgian and Congolese leaders as a useful framework for independence, a constitution closely modelled after the Belgian Constitution, this became the first Congolese constitution—the *Loi Fondamentale*. Into the *Loi Fondamentale* were hastily incorporated the political structures and norms thought appropriate to a new democratic state: a national Parliament and cabinet government, provisions for party competition and mass elections, federal apportionment of powers between national and provincial governments, an administrative apparatus, guarantees of civil liberties, and other features familiar to the Belgian system. Within months, this elaborate structure totally collapsed, ruined by the divisive cultural fragmentation which had lain dormant in Congolese political life until independence.

The Elite: Fragmentation and Ineptitude. The management of the new Congolese state fell to a leadership scarcely equipped by experience or outlook for this task.

The new political leaders possessed no coherent plan, either in ideological or operational terms, for conducting the affairs of government and setting its direction. This unpreparedness was not surprising, for the elite had been almost totally insulated from contact with national movements and leaders in other emerging nations until a few years before Congolese independence and, consequently, had scant opportunity to consult with others concerning the appropriate procedures, structures, or ends for a new state. What unity the elite possessed had been largely forged from a common resentment against the colonial power and a passion for self-determination. Additionally, political skill, trust, and collaboration were in short supply. During the colonial period, the elite had acquired its status largely through advancement into the middle administrative levels of the colonial bureaucracy—one of the few avenues of upward mobility open to natives—and lacked experience in party or organizational leadership, in the aggregating and reconciling of conflicting political goals, in the management of political campaigns and mass sentiments, and in other tasks crucial to the political vocation. Indeed, until the months immediately preceding independence, most of the new leadership had been isolated into geographic cliques with little opportunity for collaboration. Prior experience in political management and collaboration was sorely missed because the elite, like the Congolese masses, were sharply divided by ethnic, tribal, and geographic loyalties, and were suspicious toward those outside the ambit of parochial identifications; in the first years of independence, not surprisingly, it often proved a formidable task for leaders to sit together at the negotiating table. These leadership deficiencies were further compounded when decolonization rapidly absorbed the thin stratum of existing native leadership and forced the hurried recruitment of new officials with no technical or political preparation for their jobs. Within the first two years of independence, it was necessary to fill 641 new elective offices, more than 100 provincial ministries, the large central government cabinet, and approximately 10,000 top civil-service positions vacated by the Belgian exodus.

Evidence of elite fragmentation and political ineptitude was quickly manifest. During the first national elections, more than fifteen parties, reflecting the high degree of latent fragmentation among the elite, appeared in the national assembly, none commanding more than a comparatively few seats, and most badly disciplined and ideologically incoherent. In their effort to mobilize the newly enfranchised masses, party leaders commonly made extravagant promises, including immediate jobs, new prosperity, and a profusion of goods and services from government without the commensurate public costs; the failure of these goods to rapidly materialize was a major provocation of mass rejection of party activity, parliamentary government, and the leadership attempting to represent them. Public confidence in the new political leadership was further diminished by what appeared to be an immediate demonstration of parliamentary venality when the newly elected legislators, scarcely convened, voted themselves a handsome salary increase. In the end, remarked one observer, "the extraordinary circumstances of independence have served to enlarge the gap between rulers and ruled and to produce a particularly sharp sense of alienation on the part of the mass."[17]

The early failure of political leadership might have been compensated for (to the extent of maintaining some governmental stability, public order, and continuity in governmental services), if the administrative arm—long the strength of the colonial regime —had been able to function effectively. Unfortunately, the political elite usually heaped public blame for civic disorder and resentment against authority on administrators. Making no distinction between the administrative and legislative functions, legislators interfered in the most basic administrative procedures, such as the recruitment and advancement of civil servants (where personal favoritism played a large role), the management of public revenues, and much more. For their part, administrators asserted that the fanning of public resentment against them was a legislative strategy to hide its own ineptitude. The administrators found it difficult, if not impossible, to carry out their technical responsibilities and to develop the professional manpower for the job because of constant legislative meddling in the most routine administrative procedures. Soon, they became extremely suspicious of legislative intentions and wary of collaboration with "the politicians." Thus, cooperation between legislative and administrative branches, so essential in the transition to national independence, was scuttled at the outset.

From the beginning of the Congo's independence, in short, the elite political culture was a barren and inhospitable soil in which to cultivate the seeds of an effective new national government. The elite's cultural fragmentation—a compound of intense parochial outlooks, political distrust and inexperience, a highly divisive array of party platforms, and conflicting expectations for the new government's political performance—created confusion and division at the top of the political hierarchy at a time when mass political culture was wholly incapable of sustaining a national government without the most incisive and united leadership.

Mass Cultural Fragmentation. At the moment of his national independence, the average Congolese had no experience in the rules and rituals of the new "democracy" suddenly thrust upon him, and no familiarity with the freshly minted national and provincial governments suddenly supplanting the Belgian colonial regime which had regulated virtually every aspect of his life since birth. Though he might have been moved by the passionate Congolese nationalism espoused by the politicians cultivating his support for one of the numerous new parties appearing in his area, he could not easily identify with the new national government in Leopoldville, or respond with spontaneous allegiance to its symbols, officials, and pronouncements. He had suddenly become, by virtue of legal decree, a member of a "nation" which was alien to him in most instances, and a citizen in a state containing millions of other individuals with whom he was unlikely to feel any community and toward whom he quite often felt the deepest suspicion.

The lack of identification with the new political community was only one symptom of mass cultural fragmentation. Characteristically, the fragmentation of this culture involved the dominance of parochial sentiments that bonded the individual to his village, ethnic group, tribe, region, or religious sect with an intensity far exceeding his commitment to any higher political units. In particular, ethnic identifications—most often, tribal loyalties—were a persistent cause of political turmoil and disaffection from the national order. A few tribal groups, particularly the Bakango, the Congo River trading peoples (Bogangi, Lekali), and the Kasai Baluba did develop outlooks compatible with strong allegiance to a national government, but most tribal groupings did not. This intense tribalism had not been a major problem during most of the colonial regime because the outlook of the Belgian administration dominated Congolese society, and tribal political conflict could not emerge as it did when independence suddenly permitted the free play of tribal competition within the political arena.

With the coming of independence, ethnic loyalty assumed many political forms. Political parties tended to become expressions of tribal sentiments and to build their membership base upon a very narrow foundation of one, or a few, tribal groupings. Competition among candidates for elective office, party divisions in representative assemblies, the pattern of recruitment into the civil service, and almost all aspects of the political process were interpreted in terms of tribal or ethnic victories or defeats; public policy, itself, was assessed according to its tribal implications. As governmental institutions proved incapable of maintaining order, smouldering ethnic grievances often erupted into murderous violence. One concentration of ethnic hostility was in the former Kasai Province where the Kasai Baluba tribe, prosperous and dispersed throughout the region, were forced to retreat to their ethnic homeland in Sud-Kasai under the attack of other ethnic groups, particularly the Bena Lulua; the bloody exodus of the Baluba, involving perhaps 500,000 individuals, was unaccompanied by effective protection from national or provincial authorities. The separatist sentiment that produced breakaway provinces in the early years of independence is partly traceable to the attempt of ethnic groups, concentrated in specific geographic areas, to free themselves from the reign of other groups thought to dominate national politics. Eventually, the national government was forced to recognize the strength of these ethnic enclaves; in 1962, it divided the six original Congolese provinces into twenty-one to give greater local autonomy to ethnic groupings. Even this failed to arrest secessionist movements. Ethnic identification and hostility were further provoked by the problem of staffing the bureaucratic positions vacated by the Belgians; awarding of positions became an intense ethnic competition sure to provoke hostility and to sow further grievances among the groups convinced that they had lost. These ethnic tensions were magnified by the elite and, as a result, no important leadership elements existed as a countervailing force that could have buffered this divisiveness.

In addition, widespread mass resentment appeared against the "politicians" and the civil servants who did win a measure of success in the political scramble following independence. Political or administrative office could make a man quickly rich by Congolese standards and, consequently, economic grievances underlay much mass resentment, especially when thousands of citizens became public officials in the mass civil service promotions which transpired in the early years of independence. Furthermore, in July, 1961, the new government issued regulations which principally restricted the two highest civil service categories to those previously serving in the administration, almost precluding the attainment of such positions by any of the younger, university-trained Congolese, and consequently creating deep animosity toward the government among this group. Then, too, there were other accusations: the "politicians" had failed to keep the extravagant promises they had made during elections, they were too busy padding their own pockets (in mid-1962 the only significant Congolese union declared a strike against the "salaries of politicians"), they were arrogant, they were tribal, and so forth. This resentment readied a large segment of the Congolese population to mobilize against existing leaders, governmental institutions, and political formulas. This segment was organized by leaders who were themselves alienated and disappointed by their own experience in the new political game.

Against this background, the political turmoil of early Congolese independence seems almost inevitable. It is significant that a measure of stability was restored to the Congo only through the emergence of a highly authoritarian military regime, backed by a monopoly of coercive resources which, in effect, returned the Congolese to the *subject* posture they had previously experienced under the Belgian regime. Apparently, the fragmentary forces of Congolese culture are being contained through the imposition of order from above and the suppression of many political liberties, while the population is being educated, in a variety of ways, to the political orientations needed to make national independence and internal order possible. Not surprisingly, the new regime has placed heavy emphasis upon the socialization of the young, through the educational system, into a new consciousness of their national identity, and has attempted to purge the nation of many "foreign" influences in order to heighten awareness of common interests and national symbols. In a sense, the regime has been forced to begin the long process of creating an integrated political culture after the nation has already been formally fashioned, rather than building national institutions upon an existing culture appropriate to them. Whether it will succeed in this most difficult undertaking remains to be seen.

Some Larger Lessons

To study the divisive social tensions in Italy and Zaire is to transform political abstractions into contemporary history. These two countries illuminate, with particular clarity, how cultural fragmentation manifests itself in modern societies; hopefully, this brief description has helped the reader to translate the concepts included in "political fragmentation" into social realities. At the same time, a study of these two nations underlines some important conclusions about fragmented cultures generally.

In both Italy and Zaire, one can observe that fragmented political cultures are, in good measure, created or aggravated by the imposition of a national government "from above." In neither society did the national government evolve from a broadly based impulse toward political union on the part of the disparate social, geographic, and economic interests which eventually were embraced by the "nation." In neither had the national political order evolved slowly, with time for experimentation and accommodation between competing interests in an effort to create a satisfactory political formula for national existence. Rather, the national governments were established under the management of a relatively small population group; the "nations" suddenly created by this engineering of national government were artificial entities, without genuine roots in the sentiments and history of the peoples over whom they claimed sovereignty. In general, such attempts to impose national orders on a diverse population are a very fruitful source of fragmented cultures—indeed, perhaps the most frequent cause of them.

Moreover, the case studies suggest the difficulty of finding a political settlement to societal tensions so long as the social roots of the problem remain. In many respects, the chronic political tensions that mount until they threaten violence in fragmented cultures are the products of deep social disparities: between rich and poor, between educated and uneducated, between those culturally modern and those clinging to tradition. When these divisions are compounded or magnified by a population's ethnic, regional, or religious differences, it is often impossible to eliminate the resulting political tensions until the social character of the polity is altered. In this perspective, the ultimate solution to fragmented political cultures may lie as much with economic, educational, and cultural changes within the society as with any alterations in governmental forms and functions. Often, therefore, governments in fragmented political cultures must simply struggle on until the social basis for a truly integrated culture emerges, if it does.

Finally, it seems apparent that democratic political orders are so fragile in fragmented cultures that it is often impossible for a national government to function if it must follow truly liberal political norms. The problem, essentially, is that the institutions associated with democracy—freedom of expression, competitive political parties, the rule of law, limited government, and the rest—are difficult to preserve in societies where deeply divisive social tensions, broadly distributed social suspicion, and violence prevail in civic life. It is not surprising that democratic national governments have either failed (Zaire) or foundered (Italy) when attempting to manage the problems inherent in social fragmentation. It may very well be that the most effective political forms in fragmented cultures are authoritarian ones, which rely upon a large component of force to achieve civic order and which impose political norms and institutions upon dissident elements while awaiting the growth of a new generation more sympathetic to the regime.

NOTES

1. Joseph LaPolombara, *Interest Groups in Italian Politics* (Princeton: Princeton University Press, 1964), p. 62; and Joseph LaPolombara, "Italy: Fragmentation, Isolation and Alienation," in Lucian W. Pye and

Sidney Verba (eds.), *Political Culture and Political Development* (Princeton, N.J.: Princeton University Press, 1965), p. 282.

2. The economic and cultural setting of Italian politics is amply discussed in Raphael Zariski, *Italy: The Politics of Uneven Development* (Hinsdale, Ill.: The Dryden Press, 1972), chapters 1 and 2.

3. LaPolombara, "Italy: Fragmentation, Isolation and Alienation," *op. cit.*, p. 294.

4. John Clarke Adams and Paolo Barile, *The Government of Republican Italy* (Boston: Houghton Mifflin, 1966), p. 230.

5. LaPolombara, *Interest Groups in Italian Politics*, *op. cit.*, p. 58.

6. Gabriel Almond and Sidney Verba, *The Civic Culture* (Boston: Little, Brown, 1965), p. 65.

7. Zariski, *op. cit.*, p. 73.

8. Adams and Barile, *op. cit.*, p. 222.

9. LaPolombara, "Italy: Fragmentation, Isolation and Alienation," *op. cit.*, p. 290.

10. *Ibid.*, p. 293.

11. Almond and Verba, *op. cit.*, p. 79.

12. The elite-mass difference in political attitude is summarized in Giuseppe Di Palma, *Apathy and Participation* (New York: The Free Press, 1970).

13. Almond and Verba, *op. cit.*, p. 127.

14. This account of Congolese events is based largely on Crawford Young, *Politics in the Congo* (Princeton, N.J.: Princeton University Press, 1965).

15. *Ibid.*, p. 334.

16. *Ibid.*, p. 56.

17. *Ibid.*, p. 358.

5

POLITICAL CULTURE
AND PUBLIC OPINION

When the Congo erupts into a murderous civil war and massive numbers of Italians elevate tax evasion to a civic duty, it is not difficult to perceive that these manifestations of political culture are bound to effect civic life. Political violence and civil disobedience are very open, almost raw, expressions of fundamental political orientation; people directly act out their basic sentiments about government without much disguise, ambiguity, or indirection. There are many other ways, less dramatic but no less important, through which political culture seems to express itself in political affairs. Many analysts assert that political culture influences, in varying degree, most of the political sentiments we commonly group together as "public opinion"—feelings and attitudes about political candidates, parties, public issues, governmental policies, and much else—to such a degree that one cannot fully understand the impact of political culture on civic life without relating it to public opinion, whose importance must also be discussed. There are sound reasons for believing that political culture does indeed affect public opinion, even though empirical studies which demonstrate how this occurs are still scarce. A useful way to describe this relationship is to begin by distinguishing between *public opinion* and *political culture*, a necessary task because political analysts show no enthusiasm for making the distinction as clear as it might be.

SOME USEFUL DISTINCTIONS

There are almost as many definitions of "public opinion" as there are writers on the topic. The term is most often used as a shorthand for all the beliefs, values, and attitudes about political matters which might be discovered among a group of people. Here, as in our earlier discussion of political culture in chapter 1, it is helpful to be aware that different levels of analysis are involved. At the *individual* level (sometimes called the *micro* level), public opinion refers to "the individual expression of beliefs, values and attitudes about political objects."[1] At the *community* or *national* level (sometimes called the *macro* level), it refers to the manner in which various political orientations are distributed among groups of individuals. In either case, one could comfortably include within this very ample definition all the sentiments we have included in "political culture," so that political culture would be regarded as one manifestation of "public opinion."

As a practical matter, political analysts often distinguish between political culture and public opinion to emphasize that they are dealing with two different dimensions of political opinion. "Public opinion" is often used when discussing how individuals and groups are oriented toward contemporary issues, actors, and events in civic life; it is this definition we shall follow in this chapter.[2] In contrast, "political culture" refers, as we have seen, to a variety of citizen orientations toward the fundamental political institutions and processes of their political system. The major reason for making this distinction is that analysts want to have a distinctive label for those sentiments which are considered *fundamental* or *basic* to political life; implicitly, they are insisting that not all the sentiments that might be included in "public opinion" are equally critical to the stability of a political system, and those that are need the special label "political culture." This is not to suggest that the attitudes embraced by the term "public opinion" are politically unimportant, but rather that people are oriented toward different objects and institutions in political life, and that some of these orientations are more important to the fundamental political order than others.

Even though the distinction between "public opinion" and "political culture" might seem at times arbitrary (as some scholars think), it is important to recognize that citizen attitudes may have differing relevance to basic political stability. For example, it was clearly important when 75 per cent of the American public believed that President Nixon was not doing a good job in office; it could have meant the defeat of Republican candidates in congressional elections, a Democratic President in 1976, and a new direction in public policy. But, for the stability of the U.S. political system, it may be more important to know how individuals feel about the institution of the Presidency itself: Do they consider it legitimate and proper for the nation? Feelings and attitudes about contemporary political candidates and officeholders are part of the orientations we have called "public opinion." Feelings about institutions such as the Presidency we would place under the label "political culture."

We can now be more precise about the particular orientations that we shall include in "public opinion"—that is, those orientations toward contemporary issues, actors, and events in civic life that we wish to distinguish from political culture. One will discover that most public analysts would include the following orientations under this definition of "public opinion":

Party Identification—The political party (if any) to which an individual feels some degree of psychological attachment; the party to which he feels he "belongs"; (this may or may not be the party of which he is a member or in which he is registered).

Candidate Preferences—Which political candidates and officeholders an individual likes and the reason(s) for this attachment; these orientations may or may not involve any thought-out basis for the candidate preference.

Policy Preferences—An individual's feelings and attitudes concerning public policy issues; these may be issues currently important in a community or issues to which an individual feels a strong attachment regardless of their contemporary salience.

Political Information—How much an individual knows about events, actors, and institutions in his civic environment; customarily, this includes his knowledge of current officeholders, current political events, and the basic structure of his civic institutions.

Political Ideology—The degree to which an individual has an explicit, structured set of political values or attitudes that help him to interpret and respond to political events; this may involve a fairly coherent belief system (such as "conservatism" or "socialism") or a set of isolated but related beliefs.

To the student of political culture, a crucial question is how the underlying sentiments about political life, which we call "political culture," influence one's thinking about political parties, current political issues, and other affairs which constitute the common types of daily civic life. The answer to this question is important, not only because it expands our understanding of the processes through which public opinion is formed, but also because it expands our appreciation of how political culture, often subtly and unconsciously acting upon individual behavior, may profoundly affect civic life. Moreover, there is reason to assume that the path of influence flows in both directions; it is quite plausible that feelings about political affairs which we have grouped under "public opinion" can also alter basic political culture orientations.

The Impact of Political Culture. Scholars have suggested many ways in which political culture—particularly those cultural orientations acquired through early political socialization—can affect public opinion. They customarily emphasize that political culture should be thought to *influence* but not *determine* public opinion, that political culture is but one of many factors shaping adult political sentiments. We shall briefly examine several of the most important modes of influence which have been suggested.

1. *Defining the general context of opinion development and expression.* In many respects, political culture may teach a person how to form his political opinions, in what manner to express them, and to which political offices or institutions he should direct those opinions; it may teach him which political opinions are proper for him to hold and what expectations he should have about his influence in civic life.[3] In short, political culture may set the boundaries within which a citizen feels he can operate when expressing political views—that is, the culture sets the *context* although it never determines all possible opinions or behaviors. In many societies, this cultural impact will register upon a citizen only as a rather firm belief that there are ways "things are done" (or "not done") when it comes to political actions; this cultural learning may be so complete that one does not even reflect upon his mode of political thinking, taking it simply as a

"given" in life. Nonetheless, we should suspect that even opinions that seem to be formed only in response to contemporary events are underpinned by a residue of cultural influence.

Several examples will suggest how political culture may suffuse the process of political opinion formation. Perhaps an obvious illustration is that those political officials or institutions which one is taught to respect, or to trust implicitly, may have a disproportionate influence upon one's opinions on contemporary political affairs; in the United States this is particularly obvious in the case of the Presidency, where public identification with the office as a symbol of the Republic—an identification carefully and continually cultivated from earliest childhood—endows the incumbent President with enormous prestige to place in the service of those viewpoints he wishes his countrymen to adopt. In effect, the President enjoys a great initial advantage in influencing public opinion by virtue of mass cultural learning about the character of his office. Another instructive example concerns the way in which individuals may be taught to behave as "responsible citizens" when forming political opinions. In open societies where public access to a variety of political information sources is both protected and encouraged, the individual may be stimulated to listen to political argument and debate, to consult conflicting viewpoints, and to weigh issues carefully before arriving at political judgments. In closed societies, today most familiar in the Communist nations, a "responsible citizen" may be discouraged from seeking information contrary to official regime viewpoints, and may find such alternative information scarce or dangerous to solicit; he may, in fact, experience considerable anxiety and confusion if confronted with the necessity to form an opinion from conflicting viewpoints and without official cues. Citizens in two different polities may go about forming political opinions in very different manners according to how they have been taught a "good citizen" behaves. We would certainly expect that the quality of mass opinions in the contrasting societies are bound to reflect these different regime norms. More generally, even when we cannot define precisely how the culture may influence particular opinions, we have reason to believe that a variety of political culture orientations define the ways in which many people form and express political opinions, and that differences in the quality of mass opinions from one society to another may reflect, among other things, contrasting political cultures.

2. *"Screening" political information.* Political life confronts us with such a varied daily barrage of events, information, personalities, and other matters that noting and responding to them all is impossible; as with all other aspects of our experience, we tend to perceive political events selectively. Some events are noted, some ignored; some political matters are pondered, others dismissed. From the viewpoint of the political culture analyst, it is likely that political culture helps to define which kinds of political information we perceive—that is, which parts of the political world become real and meaningful to us in some manner—and, thereby, determines the information context upon which political opinions are formulated. More precisely, many analysts believe that political culture may establish psychological resistance to information incompatible with deeply held cultural values, and increase one's receptivity (or at least one's neutrality) toward information more congenial to cultural values. In some cases, political culture orientations may be so deeply meaningful to an individual that he will distort his perceptions of political realities, if necessary, to make these perceptions consistent with his political culture sentiments.

In stable political systems where a political culture compatible with the national regime is widely shared, a fundamental, extremely crucial form of screening occurs when the mass of citizens "screen out" political information that might lead to a belief that the political system should be radically changed; in such systems, it is common to find mass opinions on alternative forms of government rather poorly developed and distributed, and endorsement for revolutionary behavior very low. In general, the citizen's growth from childhood to maturity will involve some modification of early regime orientations, but a substantial core of basic loyalties and beliefs remains largely unchanged. "Early learning acts as a filter and sets broad limits on subsequent learning," concludes one scholar familiar with the matter. "It is likely (but not predetermined) that with maturation and increasing political sophistication, new information and experiences modify, but do not replace, earlier socialization; details, but not the basics, are changed."[4] In the United States and Great Britain, for example, public opinion pollsters commonly give scant attention to public sentiments concerning alternative national governmental forms because few citizens give the matter serious consideration. On a more mundane level, a citizen is most likely to have information and opinions about those levels of government with which he strongly identifies and, conversely, to give relatively little attention to those aspects of the governmental system that do not appear to be important to him. Much of this screening is, of course, unconscious, but it is to some degree a learned behavior and, therefore, one in which political socialization may have an important influence.

In another perspective, political culture is likely to teach individuals that certain leaders are more trustworthy than others, and that certain individuals are especially informed and expert on matters political by virtue of their title or position. Political culture helps to define who the opinion leaders of a society are likely to be, and arms the political elite managing the government with powerful psychological holds on public opinion and behavior. In many societies, citizens are taught from childhood that the political elite is endowed with rare wisdom and deserves public regard. A national leader may be elevated by political culture to a political paragon, and his right to be believed and obeyed become unchallengeable. In Great Britain, the Monarch symbolizes the state while the Prime Minister represents the current government. The Monarch, standing above party spirit and policy squabbles, commands great public respect and deference. The Prime Minister's portion of public trust may be less ample because he represents a party and a partisan program to which there will be opposition, but he, too, commands considerable public respect by virtue of his leadership position. In the United States, the President has customarily enjoyed great advantage in shaping public opinion by virtue of his position as Head of State as well as leader of his party; at the same time, this dual role can confront Americans with the emotional conflict generated by patriotic feelings toward the President as a national symbol and possibly intense hostility to his program and behavior as a party leader.

Because political offices, particularly at the national level, are accorded high prestige, and citizens are taught early to respect them, it is customary to discover in the United States that the holders of such office are likely to be opinion leaders on major public issues. Often, the flow of opinions from opinion leaders to the public is a two-step procedure. The opinion leaders influence the interpreters and disseminators of opinion (newspaper columnists, television reporters, and magazine writers) who, in turn, become opinion leaders to their own audience. Sometimes, political leaders are strongly influenced by this interpretive stratum of their society; there is usually some interaction between the two. In any case, the public commonly seeks "cues" in forming opinions; these cues are often provided by public officials, members of the political elite, and other figures the public has been taught to believe are the proper sources of information and interpretations on civic matters. Behind this complex process of opinion creation and transmission is likely to be the influence of political culture, structuring and perpetuating the opinions.

3. *Shaping expectations about governmental inputs and outputs.* A major task of government is the conversion of social "inputs" into policy "outputs," that is, the business of responding to demands for various policies with some authoritative policy decisions. Failure to perform this task satisfactorily may lead to prolonged social crises, pervasive social ills, and the collapse of the governmental mechanism itself. Because the policy-making process is so crucial to effective national government, political analysts have been particularly interested in the factors which determine what expectations will develop in a society regarding these "inputs" and "outputs." Many analysts believe that political culture exerts a major influence upon what demands people make upon government, upon what responses they consider to be appropriate, and upon how they believe these responses should be made.[5] Perhaps one of the most basic ways in which political culture can influence the policy-making process is by defining, for many people, the issues which are thought to be the proper responsibility of government—in effect, deciding what issues are "political" or should be "politicized." In the United States, for instance, most citizens would not readily accept the idea that

the federal government should define what constitutes "American" music and art, and then banish all "non-American" creations from the galleries, concert halls, and homes; the arts are considered outside the domain of the governmental system in American political culture. In the contemporary Soviet Union, mainland China, and in authoritarian political systems generally, citizens are taught that no social activity, including art, literature, recreation, or any other human endeavor, is beyond the political pale and that, consequently, it is proper to expect government to act in response to demands for activity in these areas. Political culture—perhaps in the form of concepts concerning the rules of the game—may also affect the kind of response segments of a polity expect from government when they make policy demands upon it. In some political systems, it is widely considered proper, under appropriate conditions, for governments to nationalize major industries or otherwise assert public control over large sectors of the economy when significant economic dislocations occur; the political "rules" do not recognize any quarantine around the economy. More dramatically, in some polities it is customary to expect governmental authorities to lash out harshly against political opponents of the incumbent regime, perhaps banishing opposition parties and expropriating their members' property; such demands, in any event, can be entertained by governmental authorities. Then, too, the *form* of demands upon government may be affected by political culture. In political cultures favorable to the formation of voluntary private associations and to political trust, by virtue of supporting cultural norms, one would expect various types of lobbying through private interest groups. In polities where such private organizations are forbidden, the lobbying may still occur but through different means. In any case, political analysts are likely to attribute to political culture a major role in shaping expectations about policy inputs and outputs.

Are such assumptions about a direct linkage between political culture and public opinion valid? To answer these questions, the investigation must move from the community to the individual level of analysis, and study how people's cultural orientations (acquired in the process of political socialization) are related to their policy likes and dislikes. Few studies have attempted this difficult task, so that any answers must be highly tentative. The absence of data reflects how recently this issue has come to interest investigators. Furthermore, it is often very difficult to obtain useful data, particularly when one is attempting to relate early political socialization to adult political opinions; reliable information from adults about their early political education—which can then be related to their current political viewpoints—is particularly hard to obtain. Interestingly, the few studies which have attempted this task suggest, contrary to what one might intuitively assume, that the link between early political socialization and adult political opinions is difficult to identify, if it exists at all. This would suggest that a child's early political socialization has little recognizable impact upon his adult political sentiments—a conclusion most scholars would reject. The data, in any case, is far too fragmentary to offer any firm conclusions, except that a strong empirical case for a linkage between childhood political education and adult political outlooks has yet to be made.

A somewhat different situation exists when one studies the relationship between the political culture orientations and other political opinions of individual adults. Generally, the most extensive research has focused upon the relationship between adult political opinions and the political orientations we have called political trust, political efficacy, and political competence. Among adults, political trust seems to be associated with a citizen's satisfaction with current governmental policies, with the kind of policy demands he makes upon government (especially with the moderateness of his policy demands), with his preference for party activity, and with expectations about future governmental performance.[6] Additionally, some studies assert that political trust strongly affects one's tolerance for governmental policy innovation, and one's willingness to delay gratifications from governmental policy outputs. All this strongly argues that political trust and distrust, however and whenever acquired, are salient structuring factors in adult policy preferences. Much the same appears true of political competence and political efficacy. Generally, individuals who score high on measures of political competence and efficacy—people who believe political activism is important and effective—are likely to be better informed about political affairs than low scorers. High scorers also tend to express political opinions more often, to be more sympathetic to a society's political norms, and to be more socially optimistic and less politically cynical than subjects who are less politically active. Thus, it appears that one cannot adequately explain the emergence of adult political opinions on many matters without some regard for the part both political efficacy and competence play in fashioning these viewpoints.[7]

These findings, lending some support to the assumption that political culture molds public opinion in important ways, indicate why the earlier propositions concerning this impact deserve careful study and testing. Moreover, the most important question about political culture is, ultimately, "What is its system impact?" Part of the answer seems to be that the impact is registered indirectly through the constant process of opinion formation, change, and expression, as well as through the direct acting out of political culture orientations and, thus, the study of political opinion in its many guises ought to be part of any effort to appreciate the full range of political culture's influence on political life. In particular, it is important to appreciate, in a general way, how political opinion, itself, influences civic life in order to understand all the ways in which political culture may ultimately express itself in political affairs.

What Political Opinion Is. Unlike the study of political culture, "public opinion" has been pondered, in various perspectives, for centuries; indeed, public opinion analysts are fond of tracing public opinion literature back to the ancient Greeks, although the material currently familiar in opinion studies (including survey research, opinion polls, computer-processed data analysis, and other modern refinements) is the product of the last thirty years. In any case, the moment we link political culture to public opinion materials we are joining a relatively new set of materials with an extremely varied, rich, and substantial body of information. The concepts, techniques, and conclusions of political opinion research have been so well developed that many conclusions can confidently be made about the effect of political opinion on civic affairs.

To begin, the term "public opinion"—an indispensable item of the scholar's vocabulary and a rhetorical staple of politicians—has been so corrupted by vague and contradictory usage that it needs clarification. Earlier, we suggested that "public opinion" could be defined as the beliefs, values, and attitudes an individual, or a large group of people, might express about contemporary political matters—a reasonable definition among many others that might be suggested. In this sense, when the political analyst studies "public opinion," he is interested only in those feelings and beliefs related to *political* matters; as far as the analyst is concerned, other opinions—about God, higher hemlines, flying saucers, or whatever—are irrelevant to his concern unless they are related by individuals to political life. It is obvious, of course, that some opinions are rather directly concerned with political affairs. A man's rating of the President, his belief about party records, or his feelings about the United Nations would be in this category. But *any* opinion can become politically relevant if an individual makes it so; this is why an important task in opinion study is to discover whether individuals do, in fact, link various opinions to civic life. For example, a strong dislike of the Catholic Church might not be primarily "political" to an observer; but if an individual— or, more significantly, a large number of people —link their religious convictions to their evaluation of Catholic candidates for political office (as millions of Protestants did during the 1960 Presidential campaign when John F. Kennedy was the Democratic candidate), the dislike becomes politically relevant to an investigator. Any opinion could conceivably become politically relevant to an individual. This underscores another important aspect of political opinion study. To understand how opinions influence political thinking and action, an investigator has to begin by examining the political world as the people he is observing see and interpret it, no matter how illogical or implausible their linkage between political opinions and behavior might seem to the "rational" observer. A conscientious investigator is concerned with how opinions are actually developed and expressed, not with how they "should" unfold.

It is also important to keep the level of analysis clear when describing public opinion. Although we can think of public opinion as an individual's orientation toward contemporary public affairs, it is most often used to refer to how a large group of individuals—a "public"—feel about such matters. Indeed, the study of public opinion is, essentially, a study of those political matters that become *public* by involving a large number of people.

When one studies political opinion (including any of the orientations included in "political culture") one result should be, as Lane and Sears have aptly suggested, a "portrait" of the opinion in several aspects.[8] A political opinion has a number of characteristics. They are

1. *Content:* the substance of the opinion; what the individual thinks or feels about the political matter under discussion
2. *Affect:* people feel strongly or weakly about a matter, they may be indifferent or intense; there is likely to be some emotional tone to the opinion which may provide a clue to its role in an individual's political life
3. *Direction:* an individual customarily "agrees" or "disagrees," feels "more" or "less" of some conviction about political affairs; it is important to know, as a rule, in which direction an opinion runs
4. *Salience:* some opinions are more important to an individual than others; generally, most people have a subjective set of opinion priorities; some opinions matter to a person a great deal, some do not, and many are between these extremes
5. *Integration:* opinions may be linked together or not; it is important to understand how one opinion is related to another —if a relationship exists—and how elaborate the linkage might be

To take a simple example, suppose an individual expresses the following viewpoint: "I believe the United States has given away too much foreign aid; this really irritates me. I'm going to vote for a candidate who will put an end to this giveaway." This can be expressed in terms of the elements in an opinion "portrait."

1. *Content:* "the United States has given away too much foreign aid"
2. *Affect:* "this really irritates me"

3. *Direction:* "too much aid"
4. *Salience:* "this really irritates me. I'm going to vote for a candidate who will put an end to this giveaway"
5. *Integration:* "I believe the United States has given away too much foreign aid [and, therefore,] I'm going to vote for a candidate who will put an end to this giveaway"

There are other dimensions into which one may fit an opinion, but these are the most common; a bit of reflection will suggest how useful—indeed, indispensable—is such information for fully understanding how and why an opinion might, or might not, influence an individual.

What Public Opinion Is Not. The manner in which public opinions are distributed among the public has become no less confused than the meaning of the term itself; frequently, the blame rests with political leaders and other public figures who manipulate the term, creating a variety of myths in the process, to suit their own purposes. While these myths will seem unconvincing when subjected to careful reflection, they are often taken for granted, or, as frequently happens, they are so concealed in a discussion of public sentiments that their existence is unrecognized. We shall examine three of the most common myths about public opinion.

The Myth of Monolithic Opinion is frequently encountered. Commonly, this appears in the guise of statements to the effect that the "public" (or the "people") thinks one thing or another or intends to do something as a result of a massive consensus upon some matter. Here, for instance, is part of a statement by a renowned political commentator upon a President's public image: "People think, too, that [the President's] adversaries are becoming too shrill, too cruel and too insatiable for revenge. They think that his enemies will not be content with an arm or a leg but wish in the most literal sense to destroy him and grind him into the dirt."[9] If an opinion poll were ever taken on this matter, it would undoubtedly reveal no such massive consensus; opinion polls almost never reveal such agreement on *any* political issue. Rather, one commonly finds that the people divide into different "publics" on most political issues. On the issue just mentioned, one public would probably agree with the columnist, another public would disagree and, if pressed further, would subdivide into various dissenting opinions, and at least some individuals would have no opinion or refuse to reveal their feelings. One can easily verify this fragmentation of public sentiment on political issues by consulting any reputable opinion poll that seeks to record accurately how a sample of the public responds to any issue posed by the interviewer. The only surprise in the fact that there are many different opinion publics on any political matter is that allegations to the contrary are often accepted as gospel.

Another frequent misrepresentation of popular sentiment can be called the *Myth of Static Opinion*. This myth assumes that opinions, once formed, are likely to be stable or virtually immutable; as people think today, so they will think tomorrow. Again, a glance at public opinion polls will quickly contradict such a facile assumption. Table 5.1 summarizes a study of a four-year trend in public ratings of local industry's efforts to control air pollution; significant fluctuations in public opinion are evident in it. One of the important tasks in the study of political opinions, including any political culture orientations, is to understand when and how opinions fluctuate and to assess the impact upon the political system. Opinions are not equally likely to vary, for some attitudes and beliefs are more resistant to change than others— party identifications in the United States and Great Britain, for instance, seem far more resistant to change, once developed, than many convictions about political issues; nevertheless, one cannot assume that any profile of public beliefs drawn at a given point in time is likely to remain substantially unaltered.

For the political culture analyst, perhaps the most important aspect of public opinion fluctuations is the extent to which they may signal a significant transformation in some aspect of political culture. For example, public approval of national political institutions often fluctuates, but so long as it returns to reasonably high levels or shows long periods of stability at high levels, the public opinion analyst would probably conclude that citizen orientations toward the institutions are generally positive. But a prolonged drop in public approval of an institution, or a pro-

TABLE 5.1

"How would you rate the job local industry has done in helping to control air pollution?"

	1967	1970	1971
Positive	29%	19%	33%
Negative	44	62	19
Not Sure	27	19	7

SOURCE: Louis Harris and Associates, cited in Hazel Erskine, "The Polls: Pollution and Industry," *Public Opinion Quarterly*, 36 (Summer 1972), 277.

tracted period of extreme disapproval, might well announce that public confidence in the institution itself has been deeply eroded, in short, that the alteration in public opinion symbolizes a transformation in political culture.

A final myth which pervades the discussion of public opinion —and perhaps the most difficult to recognize—is the *Myth of the Equal Salience of Opinions*. This is the assumption, usually implicit in a discussion, that all the opinions people hold on political life are equally important (that is, "salient") to them and that, consequently, each of their opinions will figure with equal weight in affecting their political behavior. Opinion experts know, to the contrary, that many of the beliefs expressed by the public are "doorstep" opinions formulated without much reflection or interest in response to a question concerning a matter about which the respondent may never before have thought seriously; these opinions, for the most part, seem unlikely to affect an individual's thinking or behavior very profoundly. Moreover, even if one confines attention only to those opinions people hold with some persistence, those affecting political life are often less important or influential in shaping a person's behavior than those concerned with occupation, family, social life, religious values, and other matters which preoccupy most people most of the time. Political affairs, for most people, are not important enough to merit sustained, careful thinking. Even if one concentrates solely upon political opinions, different priorities will appear. Attachments to political parties, party images, and feelings about candidates are often more critical to understanding the political behavior of the general public than issue positions. Among issues, those most likely to provoke strong feelings and opinions—that is, likely to be personally salient—are usually confined to the "bread and butter" questions of wages, working conditions, income, and other tangible concerns. It is seldom wise to assume to know which opinions are likely to be particularly salient to an individual, or a public, before study, but one can confidently predict that not all opinions held by an individual will be equally salient.

All this clarifies the type of public opinions that are most likely to interest the student of political culture. He would like to concentrate upon those opinions that are most intimately related to political behavior, and that have important consequences for the conduct of civic life; this means concentrating, most of the time, upon the salient political opinions within a polity and, hopefully, distinguishing those with long-range stability from those varying over time. Ideally, he would like to know how these opinions, if they are not part of the basic political culture orientation, are related to it. Although, as we have seen, the relationship between basic cultural orientations and other political opinions has yet to be clearly defined, it is not difficult to identify a number of political opinions with rather direct consequences for political behavior.

Public Opinion and Political Life. The impact of political opinion upon political behavior has been most thoroughly examined in the United States, Great Britain, and Western Europe, which have usually been the only polities accessible to scholars for survey research. Because most researchers have worked in societies where democratic norms are supposed to prevail, research has centered upon those opinions most strongly related to political participation generally, and voting in particular, because such activity seems so essential to the vitality of the political systems.

The Impact of Opinion on Behavior. Among the opinions apparently related to political participation and voting, none has seemed more important than party identification. The most forceful statement of this position was made in 1960 by the authors of *The American Voter* who were, in this instance, confining themselves to the American political arena. "Most Americans," they wrote, "have an enduring partisan orientation, a sense of party identification, which has wide effects on their attitudes toward the things that are visible in the political world," and this, in turn, has a "profound impact upon behavior"; these conclusions became, until recently, the orthodox interpretation of partisan identification in American life."[10]

Studies in the 1950's and 1960's strongly suggested that the strength of a person's identification with one of the major American political parties was strongly associated with how often he voted, with the depth of his interest and involvement in political life, with how much he knew about political affairs, and with the amount of political opinions he held; generally, the strong party-identifiers were likely to score highest on all these counts. The strong party-identifiers, who account for approximately one-fifth of the American electorate, were likely to settle their candidate choices early in campaigns, if there were any indecision at all; most often, it appeared, strong partisan loyalties were a device for simplifying personal interpretation and response to the political world. In effect, strong party identification resolved such important problems as defining "good" and "bad" candidates, identifying what issues to support (and on which side), and deciding when to become active in political affairs. This conclusion seemed further strengthened by evidence that a waning of party identification often brought diminishing political interest, reduced voting, and generally lowered political participation. Evidence gathered in other polities, albeit less abundant and diverse than American material, tended to confirm these conclusions about political loyalties.

Feelings about candidates themselves and about one's issue preferences also seemed important in affecting political behavior, but analysts customarily placed both these matters in a secondary position. Many interpreters asserted that issue positions were seldom a major influence upon the political behavior of most people (at least in the United States and Great Britain). In the United States and Britain, it has been common to explain an upsurge of political activism among normally apathetic citizens principally as a result of strong attraction to candidates—or, more precisely, to the "candidate image" in the mind of the citizen; the strong appeal of candidate image is also cited as the most frequent explanation for an individual's deviation from his customary party loyalty to vote for an opposition candidate. Candidate image and party identification are, for many people, strongly related, so that it is often difficult to specify which is the more important in affecting voting choices or political involvement; a preference for one party or another often colors a person's perceptions of a candidate and, conversely, an attractive candidate can sometimes add luster to his party's image in the voter's perceptions.

Until recently, opinions about political issues were commonly relegated to a distinctly minor place in any explanation of political behavior. Again, the preponderance of evidence came from the United States with some generally corroborative material from other polities. Enclaves of voters preoccupied with, and intensely committed to, specific policies or ideologies—commonly called "issue publics"—have long been identified in the United States but were commonly thought to be a relatively small portion of the electorate. Estimates in the 1950's and early 1960's suggested that perhaps 15–20 per cent of the public could be considered, by a very generous estimate, to be strongly motivated, in their voting choices and other political activities, by concern with policy questions.[11] A variety of reasons were suggested for the apparently weak impact of issues upon political behavior, including low public involvement in politics generally, the abstractness and remoteness of many political issues to most people, the confusion and difficulty people experience in attempting to understand where candidates stand on issues, and other reasons; in general, issue thinking seemed difficult and unappealing to most people. Thus, most interpreters of American political behavior tended to stress the role of party loyalties and candidate images when discussing those political opinions most directly linked to political activities.

As the 1960's progressed, however, this view came under increasingly heavy criticism in the United States, where a variety of studies suggested a new public issue-consciousness was developing, with a resulting upsurge in issue-motivated political activism and candidate selection. Since these findings appeared at the same time as other data pointing to an apparent decrease in the strength and frequency of party identification among the public, the conclusion seemed warranted that the American electorate was producing a much larger "issue public" than before and that, consequently, issue thinking had to be given greater weight among the factors affecting political behavior than had previously been assumed.[12] This era of "issue salience," many interpreters argued, was triggered by the major political events of the 1960's—political assassinations, civil disobedience, violence sparked by racial conflict, the saturation of the media with news of the savage and inconclusive Indo-China War, and other highly disturbing events forced upon public attention. Then, too, candidates felt compelled to discuss and clarify issues to a greater degree than seemed true of the 1950's, so that the public was being educated into issue thinking by its political leadership. Young voters, in particular, seemed preoccupied with such issues as the Indo-China War, morality in government, civil rights, and other matters, even though their own party identifications were not well formed; they were not only an "issue public" of importance, but one which would, apparently, increasingly shape the character of the electorate as the voting age was lowered and the young gradually replaced older generations. The newly emergent issue public may, in fact, be related to the depth of political culture orientations among the American public and particularly among the young. In many respects, the newer, issue-oriented voters were protesting what they believed to be a betrayal of traditional American values and institutional practices, and were demanding a return to policies and processes often associated with basic political culture values: government by majority, protection of minority rights, the rejection of political violence, and other principles exalted during the basic political socialization of most Americans.

If this reasoning is correct—and the evidence is tentative—then it will be necessary to reassess the previous interpretations of political behavior and, perhaps, to elevate "issue publics" to greater importance.

The stress placed on party loyalty, candidate appeal, and issues as the principal influences on political behavior does not mean that other attitudes and beliefs are irrelevant to political behavior, or that these three factors develop independently of other influences. It is well known, for instance, that in almost all political systems about which we have reliable survey data, political activism and other evidence of political involvement are strongly associated with educational attainment and social status. In societies where opportunities for political expression may be formally or informally controlled according to race, religion, or other social characteristics, it is predictable that political behavior will vary significantly according to the social characteristics of individuals. Since the opinions which affect political behavior do not develop apart from other influences, investigators are constantly seeking to identify the factors which seem most critical in shaping these important opinions. In particular, political institutions of several kinds appear to exert considerable influence upon political opinions which, in turn, strongly affect behavior; we can examine a few of these important institutions.

Political Institutions and Political Opinions. To the question "Why do people think as they do politically?" the public opinion analyst is likely to answer, in good measure, "because of the social institutions with which they live." Individuals are not always alert to this influence, even though they may recognize that social institutions create the basic design of their daily lives; much of this political influence is subtle and indirect but nonetheless effective. We have already noted that family and school actively participate in forming a young person's view of his political system, his role in it, and his political loyalties; by the time most citizens are mature enough to examine their own political values, they may have assimilated many political opinions conveyed through family and school so completely that these opinions seem to be givens, indisputable beyond argument. Almost all the institutions which absorb much of an individual's time and interest —family, vocation, and group associations among them—will contribute something to his political viewpoints. Among these, there are several political institutions likely to figure predominantly in his political thinking.

In most political systems, *the norms governing political expression*—particularly those defining who may participate in political life and under what rules—will influence a citizen's view of the political world. In political systems where political privileges are tied to membership in a political party (as is the case in totalitarian systems where party membership is usually a condition for enjoying privileges), a person's concepts of his own political influence, of his sympathy for the political regime, and of his involvement in political affairs are likely to depend upon whether he is a party member. Where political discrimination is actively practiced toward distinct social groups, as was the case in the American South toward blacks and which occurs in many other political systems, where many different social groups are the target of discrimination, those bearing the burden are likely to differ from other social groups regarding a variety of opinions relating to political life. In the United States, for instance, opinion studies customarily reveal that blacks, Mexican-Americans, and members of other minority groups enduring political discrimination tend to be more cynical, less optimistic, and more impatient with the progress of political reform than other social groups. Not surprisingly, the issues which preoccupy the attention of the disfavored groups tend to be those associated with their own political circumstances. The norms defining who may participate in political life, and how—which, in effect, declare who "belongs" in the political system and to whom the system will be most responsive—usually create different political realities for different social groups, and we would expect differing opinion climates to develop in such frequently contrasting political climates.

In addition, the *nature of the political party system* is likely to exert a continuing sway on the development and expression of public opinions. This is particularly true in regard to the development of party identification, party images, and responses to party leaders. In the United States and Great Britain, for instance, where two-party systems have prevailed at virtually every major political level for almost a century, voters almost always develop loyalties to one of the major parties and resist attachment to third parties, except under unusual circumstances, which rarely cause long-term changes in affiliation. In cases where one-partyism is the rule—in constituencies where only one party can seriously contest an election or (as in the American Southern states) where one party has been regionally dominant—citizen loyalties may be tied exclusively to that party; individuals, in effect, are socialized into accepting their party identification, in part, by the absence of any viable alternatives. In contrast, where multi-partyism prevails (as in France and the Scandinavian countries), one is likely to find not only a diversity of party loyalties within a given constituency but, perhaps, a greater range of viewpoints on political issues resulting from the greater number of party perspectives available to the citizen. In totalitarian systems, the regime may tolerate only a single state party embodying the dominant regime ideology and led by the political elite; in such instances, citizens are customarily socialized to accept the programs as the only acceptable political orthodoxy, the party propaganda as the only legitimate cues to citizens in formulating opinions, and the activities of the party as the only correct expression of citizen political goals. If this socialization is effective, citizen opinions may be largely determined, or powerfully shaped, by party perspectives, and civic moods may be largely responsive to changing party outlooks. Although totalitarian parties rarely succeed in socializing their citizenry to such an extent that they can effectively control almost all mass political attitudes, studies in the Soviet Union, mainland China, and Nazi Germany indicate a high degree of opinion manipulation and control can be achieved by skillful party leaders in a one-party system.

Finally, we should re-emphasize the role of *political socialization*—essentially a responsibility of the state—in forming early, enduring political opinions. Not only political culture orientations but issue positions and numerous policy preferences among adults are probably rooted in early childhood learning. In the United States, for instance, "opinions formed on such topics as foreign involvement, civil rights, and the government's economic role may have their roots in this [socialization] period. . . . In certain broad issue areas, individuals tend to operate within bounds set by earlier political socializations."[13] If one thinks of political socialization in broader terms than formal education experiences, including within the concept the unintended learning that individuals often receive from watching the political behavior of public officials (police, judges, local elected officials, etc.), or the opinions and attitudes acquired in the family but originating in the unofficial political norms of a community (such as tacit discriminatory acts against minorities), then the impact of socialization upon later adult political attitudes must be considered quite important. Indeed, many political scientists speak of communities as possessing an "educational climate" in which many norms for political behavior and thinking are unofficial, even unwritten, but nonetheless widely operative and understood; these are taught to youngsters informally or formally, in a manner which often has a more enduring impact than the official norms the schools are "supposed" to advocate. Many of these unofficial norms and "climates" are largely created, or perpetuated, through political officials and public agencies. Although our knowledge of the impact of political socialization upon adults is very fragmentary in the case of most non-Western countries (and totalitarian ones, especially), one would expect socialization to include a very broad range of policy positions which children are expected to embrace and perpetuate through adulthood.

Conclusions. Political culture orientations are expressed in a multitude of ways, including the responses of citizens to political parties, current policy issues, elections, other topics of current political interest, and public officials. Since the impact of political culture on political systems is often diffused through many types of public opinion, an important task in the study of political culture is to identify, if possible, how these cultural orientations are linked to current public attitudes in a political system. Research on this topic is still quite incomplete and much remains to be discovered. However, any understanding of the long-range consequences of political culture for political stability and change within political systems must take into account this culture-opinion linkage.

NOTES

1. James J. Best, *Public Opinion* (Homewood, Ill.: The Dorsey Press, 1973), p. 3. The discussion of these definitional problems extends from page 1 to 48.
2. In addition to Best, *op. cit.*, other examples of this distinction are Robert S. Erikson and Norman R. Luttbeg, *American Public Opinion* (New

York: John Wiley and Sons, 1973); and Bernard C. Hennessy, *Public Opinion*, 2nd ed. (Belmont, Calif.: Wadsworth Publishing Co., 1970).

3. See Richard E. Dawson and Kenneth Prewitt, *Political Socialization* (Boston: Little, Brown, 1969), chapters 2, 4–6.

4. Robert Weissberg, *Political Learning, Political Choice and Democratic Citizenship* (Englewood Cliffs, N.J.: Prentice-Hall, 1974), p. 28.

5. A thorough statement of these orientations is found in Gabriel Almond and C. Bingham Powell, Jr., *Comparative Politics: A Developmental Approach* (Boston: Little, Brown, 1966), chapters 1–6.

6. For two recent studies confirming this conclusion, see Jack Citrin, Herbert McClosky, J. Merrill Shanks, and Paul M. Sniderman, "Personal and Political Sources of Political Alienation" (Paper presented at the American Political Science Association Convention, New Orleans, September 4–9, 1973); and Joel D. Aberbach and Jack L. Walker, *Race in the City* (Boston: Little, Brown, 1974).

7. On the relationship between opinion holding and other psychological variables, see Almond and Verba, *op. cit.*, chapter 9; and Robert E. Lane and David O. Sears, *Public Opinion* (Englewood Cliffs, N.J.: Prentice-Hall, 1964), chapter 6.

8. Lane and Sears, *op. cit.*, chapter 1.

9. William S. White, *Washington Post*, April 13, 1974.

10. Angus Campbell, Philip E. Converse, Warren E. Miller, and Donald E. Stokes, *The American Voter* (New York: John Wiley and Sons, 1964), p. 273.

11. *Ibid.*, chapter 9.

12. Richard E. Dawson, *Public Opinion and Contemporary Disarray* (New York: Harper and Row, 1974), chapters 3 and 6.

13. Donald J. Devine, *The Political Culture of the United States* (Boston: Little, Brown, 1972), p. 148.

6

FOUR ENDURING ISSUES

All political cultures, no matter how stable or integrated, are submitted to constant stress. Dynamic forces are always active within political systems, creating tensions that must somehow be managed, challenging the skill of political leaders, and testing the resiliency of the political culture. All the forces generating tension and change within a political culture are potentially disruptive, particularly if they are unrecognized or if political leaders fail to assess the implications of change realistically. The situations generating social tension within political systems are commonly a mixture of events unique to a specific culture and of those common to most cultures. In this chapter we are concerned with four potentially disruptive problems found, with varying severity, within most political systems. None of these situations necessarily leads to major political disorder or political culture disintegration, but they can, under the proper circumstances, trigger major political problems and major political culture disorders.

ELITE-MASS CULTURE CLEAVAGES

There is frequently a major difference in political culture orientations between the elite and the masses of a political system. This disparity seems to assume two general patterns, one found predominantly in the developing nations, the other in the Westernized, democratic systems. Although these patterns differ as to the extent of cultural disassociation between elite and masses, either cleavage may produce severe civic stress unless managed skillfully.

Variation I: Modernizing Elite and Traditional Masses. Newly developing countries, especially postcolonial ones, have often begun the struggle for nationhood with an enormous gulf separating the political elite and masses—not only a discontinuity in political orientations, but a deep, pervasive difference in the most fundamental cultural attitudes, values, and styles. This cleavage arises from the manner in which the political elites were socialized, educated, and recruited.[1] Commonly, the native political elite in a newly emergent nation was educated in Westernized schools (often in Europe or the United States during the collegiate years) and quickly adopted Western viewpoints. "In dress, in recreations, in tastes in food and drink, and, much more importantly, in their attitude toward what is valuable in life," writes one observer, "they diverge considerably from the ordinary members of their societies. Even though they wear their traditional garments on ceremonial and festive occasions they wear modern clothing in the daily working life."[2] Once educated, this Westernized elite was usually recruited into the colonial administration and otherwise groomed for whatever leadership roles were available for the native political class under colonial control. Instead of following the role assigned them by their European superiors, this elite often became the spearhead of insurrection against the colonial regime, including the writers and speakers who proclaimed the end of colonialism while rallying the masses behind programs of freedom and independence from European domination, and the organizers of violence and protest in the course of native emancipation.

The elites may have framed their opposition to colonialism in terms of both native rights and the importance of cultural autonomy, but they had distinctly Western concepts of where they intended to lead the newly liberated nations—toward "modernization." Modernizing closely corresponded to what the elite believed had been achieved in the most advanced Western nations. It meant that social change should be welcomed—indeed, deliberately fostered—and tradition rejected, as a fundamental social principle. It meant that the nation must develop a widespread, participatory democracy, complete with the necessary electoral system and political party organizations. For a govern-

ment to be "modern" meant possessing the authority and resources to penetrate the society sufficiently to generate the wealth
necessary to produce the welfare state benefits needed by the
masses. Modernization also implied economic independence, if
possible, from the major powers; this could only be achieved
through rapid industrialization, the development of urban cultures, and a specialized work force attuned to the manpower
needs of a modern economy. A modern state meant mass education intended to socialize the masses into the outlooks and values
associated with advanced countries. And, most of this depended
upon creating and maintaining a strong, national government
with sovereignty over its territory. In short, the leadership mantle
in the newly emergent states fell to those who brought an essentially Western viewpoint to the task of nation building.

In virtually all the new states, however, the modernizing elite
confronted masses deeply attached to traditional society in both
form and philosophy; this majority—customarily peasant—consti-
tuted an inert, resistant culture, unwilling to bend easily in the
direction ordained by the new leadership. The masses often possessed vague and uninspiring concepts of the nation and its government, resented and resisted efforts to modernize their traditional folkways and working style, and found new party leaders
and symbols alien. Sometimes, masses who had been rallied for a
while to the program of the new leadership became disillusioned
and withdrew when the rewards expected from political participation failed to materialize quickly or the high cost of modernization became apparent. Parochial loyalties, especially, failed to
yield to appeals for a truly national outlook and a national vision
of the political community. Thus, a fundamental tension was in-
troduced into the social framework of the political system, a tension between traditional and modern cultures which overlay a
cleavage between elite and masses.

On the psychological level, this incompatability of cultures
often produced elite impatience and alienation from the masses,
complicating the elite's quest to identify with, and lead, the people. On the other side, large portions of the masses often became
embittered or indifferent toward the political programs of the
elite, or rebelled in various ways against elite leadership for rea-

sons often traceable to a rejection of modernization. At the political level, the elite-mass culture differences often led to major problems. Early attempts at participatory democracy, widespread political party activities, and other expressive freedoms associated with democracy often produced violence, civil war, or other civic ills when the masses (and sometimes segments of the elite) failed to accept the peaceful settlement of conflict, the right of majorities to rule, or the political triumph of other social groups. Often, the masses grew angry and impatient when the political elite failed to produce immediate rewards for political activism. Mass parochial sentiments often frustrated the elite's effort to mobilize human and material resources for the central government. Elaborate plans for industrialization sometimes foundered when mass cooperation failed to materialize voluntarily. Newly emergent nations varied in the breadth of the gap between mass and elite and in the gravity of the resulting problems, but few nations were able to maintain the elaborate framework of constitutional democracy and the ambitious timetable of modernization drafted in the immediate aftermath of independence.

One possible resolution of the elite-mass culture gap was for elites to ease their pressure for modernization by relaxing timetables for industrialization, by allowing a longer period for national loyalties to develop among the population, and by placing greater reliance upon compromise and negotiation as techniques for dealing with traditionalist resistance to change.[3] More often, however, modernizing elites could not, or would not, slacken the pace of modernization. One common result was decay of the original democratic constitutional order as the leadership classes found it impossible to achieve their ends while preserving mass participation in the political system. This movement away from participatory democracy often resulted in the growth of national strong men, sometimes in the guise of charismatic leaders, who succeeded in gaining an authoritarian control over the political system; this pattern occurred in Ghana and Egypt, for example. Sometimes the military seized the government and ran it largely as a military oligarchy. On other occasions, a modernizing oligarchy combining party leaders and civil servants ran the country while paying little more than lip service to democratic principles.

What these solutions shared was the emergence of a strongly authoritarian regime, backed by coercive force, which succeeded in imposing a semblance of modernization upon a traditionally-oriented mass. Occasionally (as in India), modernizing elites could proceed while preserving a significant measure of democratic practice within the political system, but these situations were relatively rare.

Authoritarian regimes arising from the collapse of democratic experiments often defend their approach as a necessary, but only temporary, measure, to be gradually eliminated as the masses are socialized into a truly modern social outlook and develop a greater ability to accept the terms of a democratic order. Yet, such elites often show little enthusiasm for making this transition —if, indeed, they are even rhetorically committed to it—with the result that liberal elements in many of the newer nations have resorted to agitation, violence, or guerilla tactics in efforts to force a greater democratization of political systems firmly controlled by authoritarian elements. It is far too early to determine if any characteristic historic patterns will emerge from these confrontations between modernizing elites and traditional masses; as we have seen, the short-range consequences seem to be a large measure of internal disorder, a resort to authoritarian rule as a solution, and the decay of internal democracy.

Variation II: Democratized Elite and Ambivalent Mass. Some analysts conclude from their study of the voluminous materials on American political opinion that there is a fundamental cleavage between the nation's political elite and masses when it comes to understanding and accepting the democratic norms supposed to govern the country's political life. So pronounced is the difference, suggest these commentators, that elite and masses are two different subcultures in terms of their democratic orientations. Scattered evidence from other Western democracies suggests that such discontinuity of political outlooks may pervade most democratic systems.

According to this reasoning, studies comparing political attitudes of elites (political officeholders, activists, and opinion leaders) with the general population commonly reveal that the elite expresses greater consensus upon abstract democratic values and

TABLE 6.1

Political Influentials vs. the Electorate:
Response to Items Expressing Support for Specific Application
of Free Speech and Procedural Rights

Item	Political Influentials (N = 3,020)	General Electorate (N = 1,484)
	Percentage Who Agree	
Freedom does not give anyone the right to teach foreign ideas in our schools.	45.5	56.7
A man oughtn't to be allowed to speak if he doesn't know what he's talking about.	17.3	36.7
A book that contains wrong political views cannot be a good book and does not deserve to be published.	17.9	50.3
When the country is in great danger we may have to force people to testify against themselves even if it violates their rights.	28.5	36.3
No matter what crime a person is accused of, he should never be convicted unless he has been given the right to face and question his accusers.	90.1	88.1
If a person is convicted of a crime by illegal evidence, he should be set free and the evidence thrown out of court.	79.6	66.1
If someone is suspected of treason or other serious crimes, he shouldn't be entitled to be let out on bail.	33.3	68.9
Any person who hides behind the laws when he is questioned about his activities doesn't deserve much consideration.	55.9	75.7
In dealing with dangerous enemies like the Communists, we can't afford to depend on the courts, the laws and their slow and unreliable methods.	7.4	25.5

SOURCE: Herbert McClosky, "Consensus and Ideology in American Politics," *American Political Science Review*, 58 (June, 1964), 367.

greater ability to translate these values into appropriate practices. The elites are not simply better informed, more active, or more interested in civic affairs; they more closely approximate the ideal modern democratic citizen in basic political attitudes than do the masses. Such conclusions are reached on the basis of survey findings akin to those illustrated in Table 6.1, which compares the response of American "political influentials" with those of a sample of the general electorate on questions dealing with support for free speech and other procedural freedoms protected by the Constitution. The "influentials" tend to make the appropriate democratic response with far greater frequency than the general electorate. Based upon such material, some commentators depict American political culture in terms of two sharply different culture milieus. In the elite milieu, a generally liberal, tolerant, democratic outlook prevails. According to one analyst:

> The political views of the influentials are relatively ordered and coherent. As liberals and conservatives, Democrats and Republicans, they take stands on issues, choose reference groups, and express preferences for leaders that are far more consistent than the attitudes and preferences exhibited by the electorate. . . . The evidence suggests that it is the articulate classes rather than the public who serve as the major repositories of the public conscience and as the carriers of the [Democratic] Creed.[4]

In contrast, the average American may not be an anti-democrat, but he is likely to be an ambivalent democrat, irresolute in his dedication to democratic values and quite erratic when applying democratic norms to concrete situations where, according to many interpreters, the real test of such values must be made. The aforementioned analyst concludes:

> The findings furnish little comfort for those who wish to believe that a passion for freedom, tolerance, justice and other democratic values springs spontaneously from the lower depths of society. . . . Even in a highly developed democratic nation like the United States, millions of people continue to possess only the most rudimentary understanding of democratic ideology.[5]

Some analysts have drawn provocative, often highly controversial conclusions from such data. It is sometimes asserted, for instance, that a healthy democratic system may depend upon control by the elite, whose orientations are most likely to assure at least a minimum of democratic practice. To place the management of civic life in the hands of the ambivalent masses, by whatever procedure, would be to invite a far greater abuse of democratic norms, if it did not introduce a large dose of anti-democratic sentiment into major political institutions. Moreover, some commentators have suggested, as a corollary to this argument, that democracy in the United States is most secure when there are relatively modest levels of participation in elections, and when the elite is given generous latitude to operate, unencumbered by the need for constant mass consultation and legitimation before making major decisions. In this perspective, "participatory democracy"— which usually implies high mass involvement in virtually all major political processes, and a limited deference to the elite—might well operate at the expense of traditional democratic freedoms. According to some analysts, the process of recruitment into the political elite involves a type of socialization, by formal and informal means, into a liberal democratic outlook which the average American has neither the time nor interest to acquire. Given these conditions, one frequently asserted conclusion is that it is unwise, if not dangerous, to politicize the masses.

This two-culture interpretation has been challenged in a number of ways.[6] It has been asserted that the survey questions usually used to compare mass and elite attachment to democratic norms do not offer reliable predictions of how people will actually behave, nor do they necessarily measure attitudes correctly. Also, it has been asserted that the political behavior of elites—to the degree that it is possible summarily to identify the values contained in their enormous variety of behaviors—do not prove that they embrace democratic values more fervently or perceptively than the masses. Indeed, it has been suggested that political elites are, by virtue of education, experience, and greater political information, often more clever in concealing their nondemocratic outlooks than are the masses. Critics of American political institutions, especially those who believe the nation is manipulated against the interests of the masses by a political and economic elite, have been particularly incensed by suggestions that the average citizen is to be trusted less to protect democracy's values than the elite. They argue that the political elite (which is likely to be part of the economic elite) has historically been committed to more anti-democratic behavior (though officially pronouncing democratic pieties) than have the average citizens. The debate continues, at the level of techniques and conclusions, concerning the validity of the elite-mass interpretation of American political culture. Those who largely accept the distinction between the two cultures are prone to contend that American democracy has worked, and continues to work, largely because the political system is managed by a democratic elite, while those who reject these cultural arguments are not alarmed by the suggestion that the existing elite might be displaced to a great extent through some form of greater participatory democracy.

POLITICAL SUBCULTURES

Though arguments about the difference between elite and mass political orientations in the United States remain inconclusive, the discussion illuminates another situation that is almost always found in political systems. Political systems may not necessarily divide nicely into elite and mass. Instead, they usually contain a number of *subcultures* that raise constant problems of political management and can sometimes be extremely disruptive to the system itself. So familiar a phenomenon are subcultures in comparative political analysis that their existence can almost be predicted in the course of studying virtually any political system.

A Common Phenomenon. In the simplest terms, a political subculture is an aggregation of individuals within a political system whose political orientations differ significantly from the great majority within the culture or, at least, vary from the cultural orientations dominant in the society. Of course, one cannot draw any sample of individuals from a political culture without discovering some variation from the majority in their political orientations; it is equally likely that almost any major social grouping within a political system will betray some attitudes or values at variance with the rest of the society, or different from the official norms. A social group called a political subculture is distinguished by relatively large membership, by important differences in outlook from the national majority, and by strong group consciousness of its difference—a difference the larger society often regards with considerable unease, if not hostility.

Subcultures are seldom politically significant if they are small in relation to the larger population, if their numbers are widely dispersed through a political system, or if the individuals do not strongly identify with the subculture. Thus, religious dissidents, such as the Amish in the United States, the extreme orthodox Jews in Israel, or remnants of Mohammedan cults in the Soviet Union, pose no serious political problems, though their political orientations are likely to be severely at odds with the dominant political cultures; such subcultures are too small and fragmented to be politically disruptive. The Scots in Great Britain and the native Indians in Brazil, though significant portions of their national populations in number and somewhat at odds with the dominant political cultures, are widely dispersed and lack the strong group cohesiveness sufficient to produce political tension with the dominant cultures of their societies.

Subcultures assume more importance when they are populous, particularly when the membership is concentrated geographically within a certain area, such as a city, a set of communities, or a state or region, and when the members share a number of social characteristics—race, religion, social status, occupation, or other distinguishing features. These conditions intensify a group's cohesion by magnifying a member's awareness of his group membership; it is easier for him to think of "we" when the group is a daily, visible reality and the shared characteristics obvious. Under such conditions, groups are likely to cling strongly to their own political orientations because there is group reinforcement and reward for such behavior.

The Pervasiveness of Political Subcultures. One can understand why political subcultures often exist in a state of tension with dominant political cultures by examining briefly the orientations which usually set subcultures apart from the rest of a society. Members of subcultures are likely to share one or more of the following orientations:

Nationalist sentiments conflicting with the existing national government. The members may feel their primary allegiance is to another national government, or may regard the existing national government as illegitimate. This can happen when populations are forcibly incorporated within a political system, or when they become part of an occupied territory or satellite state. These nationalist sentiments sometimes show amazing tenacity, lasting for generations despite great animosity and repression from the dominant national regime.

Intense and numerous parochial loyalties. Although these parochial subcultures are, as we have seen, particularly common in the developing countries, they occur in many other political systems. The most common form of parochialism is a traditionalist subculture within a modern, or modernizing, society—quite commonly, a peasant, rural subculture. However, parochial subcultures can also take form about religious, ethnic, or racial groupings. What such subcultures commonly share is a commitment to political values and procedures incompatable with, or hostile to, the dominant political norms of the society.

Folkways objectionable to the dominant culture. Conflict between culture and subculture may erupt over differences in life styles, or economic problems, and then become politicized in an effort to resolve the conflict. In India and Canada, for instance, conflicts between the central government and subcultures quite commonly occur over language; the subcultures insist upon using indigenous languages in schools, and in governmental and commercial operations, while central authorities insist upon standardizing the national language through the elimination or discouragement of regional tongues.

Extreme political alienation leading to secessionist movements. Subcultural groups do not necessarily develop secessionist sentiments —such a move may be impossible—but agitation for political secession is often the result of prolonged conflict between subcultures and the dominant political culture. These secessionist movements, commonly involving geographic groups seeking to establish an independent state or to join an adjacent state, are likely to be most vigorous and successful in the early stages of nation building, when many new states lack strong central governments. However, secessionist areas may prevail for many generations in a nation, and may (as the American South indicates) succeed in their separatist goals after long agitation.

Political subcultures are found in most political systems. They appear in such divergent forms as the blacks in the United States, the French of Canada, the Bengalese in Pakistan, the Tibetans in China, and the Indians in Uganda. Subcultures are best known in political systems where access to information and official ideologies permit extensive investigation, but there is considerable indirect evidence of major subcultural disturbances in many totalitarian systems despite regime dedication to eliminating opposition and frequent assertions of internal harmony. The Soviet Government, for instance, has fought against dissident subcultures constantly—not only among its Eastern European allies, where strong anti-Soviet nationalism endures, but within the borders of the Soviet Union, where Moscow's hegemony is assumed. Expressions of nationalist sentiment from any of the republics within the Soviet federation, or even a hint of it, can bring quick censure from the central government, even when the sentiments are hardly revolutionary. Poets and writers in the central Asian republic of Kirghizia, for instance, have been reprimanded by the Kremlin for dwelling overlong upon their snowy mountains and other regional beauties, lest they be glorifying the pre-Soviet past and the traditional folkways of a country whose people, mostly Turkic-speaking and physically akin to the Mongols, once enjoyed independence from Soviet influence. During World War II, the Ukraine might have joined Hitler's Reich after German troops temporarily liberated it from Soviet domination, for Ukranians were a fiercely independent people who did not accept Moscow's domination easily and who sought greater regional autonomy. Nazi brutality against the civilian population, however, rapidly destroyed any separatist sentiments and drove most Ukranians back into the Soviet camp. A number of other Soviet states continue to be restive, such as the state of Georgia, where the inhabitants exhibit a robust regional independence and pride that sits poorly in Moscow.

The two most familiar American subcultures are those of Southerners and of blacks. The Southern subculture, which grew out of historic differences from the rest of the Union in economy, life style, and political elite values, was primarily a regional, white subculture with strong secessionist inclinations which reached their most potent expression in the events precipitating the Civil War.[7] Since then, the region has differed from the rest of the nation in terms of its preference for extensive political autonomy and freedom from federal government authority, its one-

TABLE 6.2

Children's Evaluation of the President Within Three Subcultures
(Grades Five Through Eight)

Question	Response	Texas Chicanos	Appalachians	Chicagoans
1. View of how hard the President works compared with most men	Harder	49%	35%	77%
	As hard	27	24	21
	Less hard	24	41	3
		100%	100%	101%
	N =	48	128	214
2. View of the honesty of the President compared with most men	More honest	*	23%	57%
	As honest	*	50	42
	Less honest	*	27	1
			100%	100%
	N =		133	214
3. View of the President's knowledge compared to most men	Knows more	41%	45%	82%
	Knows about the same	42	33	16
	Knows less	17	22	2
		100%	100%	100%
	N =	62	124	212
4. View of the President as a person	Best in the world	11%	6%	11%
	A good person	63	68	82
	Not a good person	26	26	8
		100%	100%	101%
	N =	37	139	211

* Data not reported.

SOURCE: Robert Weissberg, *Political Learning, Political Choice and Democratic Citizenship* (Englewood Cliffs, N.J.: Prentice-Hall, 1974), p. 52. Appalachian and Chicago data reported in Dean Jaros, Herbert Hirsch, and Frederic J. Fleron, Jr., "The Malevolent Leader: Political Socialization in an American Sub-Culture," *American Political Science Review*, 62 (June, 1968), 568; the Mexican-American data are reported in Herbert Hirsch and Armand Gutierrez, "The Socialization of Political Aggression and Political Affect: A Subcultural Analysis," unpublished paper.

partyism, its extremely repressive social and political controls over native blacks, its predominantly agricultural and rural folkways, and many other things. This regionalism seems to be eroding in the wake of rapid industrialization, regional immigration, civil rights gains among blacks, growing public education, and the nationalizing effect of the media. American blacks, it has long been known, commonly view political realities in different terms than whites. Blacks are usually more reserved in their approval of governmental performance, less optimistic and trusting toward public officials, more skeptical of governmental promises, and generally less convinced that the liberal democratic norms supposed to govern political life actually do so—understandably, given their long experience of discrimination.[8] There are other significant subcultures, however. One interesting depiction of them is found in Table 6.2, which compares the responses of Appalachian and Chicano school children with those of a cross-section of Chicago youngsters on questions dealing with the President's competence and behavior. (Researchers believe that the attitudes of grammar school children toward the President reflect the political climate of the home and tap more diffuse attitudes toward national government generally.)

These data, reflecting significantly lower confidence in the President among Chicano and Appalachian youngsters compared to the Chicago sample, reflects the social experience of the three groups. Mexican-American children, like young blacks, feel early and continually the weight of discrimination historically directed toward their parents within American society, and respond toward major public officials in a similar manner. Appalachian children live within the most economically depressed region of the United States, among a subculture which has a long history of suspicion toward most agencies of government, and which is becoming increasingly dependent upon public welfare and, consequently, embittered.

The Making and Unmaking of Subcultures. For anyone concerned with political culture, perhaps the most important questions about political subcultures concern the reasons for their development and the manner in which they are treated within political systems.

Two very common reasons for the existence of subcultures are the conquest of one state by another and the co-optation of populations into a state during nation building. The creation of subcultures by conquest is most visible today in Eastern Europe, where such previously sovereign states as Poland, Czechoslovakia, and Hungary have been reduced to Soviet satellite governments. While a varying measure of political, economic, and cultural freedom is permitted, Russian tolerance for "deviationism" is limited, and national sovereignty in any of the older Eastern European countries is largely a pretense. Nonetheless, nationalism still smoulders below the surface of Soviet hegemony in Eastern Europe, occasionally leading to civil war between satellite nationalists and Soviet representatives (as in Hungary in 1954 and Czechoslovakia in 1970), and appearing in stubborn resistance to the cultural leveling by which the Soviet government attempts to destroy traditional cultural institutions. Populations forced into subcultural conditions by conquest often endure and sometimes prosper over extraordinarily long periods without losing their sense of uniqueness or their disaffection from the dominant culture; the French Canadians and Irish, for example, have existed for centuries within political systems to which they were never reconciled completely. Many subcultures have been created during the last thirty years in the newer states of Africa and Asia. As we saw in the case of the Congo, a very volatile situation can be produced when strong political and cultural dissimilarities exist between the national culture and subculture. Such tensions are often a direct result of the nation-building process, where an attempt is made to build a political community from geographically contiguous elements, sharing no strong national sentiments, who co-existed in reasonable peace under a colonial government only because most expressions of cultural autonomy were suppressed. With liberation from colonial rule, however, it was inevitable that some cultural element, or coalition of elements, should dominate the new national governments and become the major political culture components; this frequently inspired other subcultures, themselves ambivalent about the new nation, to seek greater autonomy, often by threatening or attempting secession. Even today, more than three decades into the postcolonial era, it has been estimated that almost all the new nations of Africa and Asia still contain important secessionist elements.

Sometimes, political subcultures are created by the immigration of new cultural groups into established political cultures. If this immigration is largely voluntary, conflict between culture and subculture tends to be minimized, and the subculture may exist as a distinctive social entity, exhibiting many cultural idiosyncrasies without strong political resistance to dominant political norms. This was the case among most of the white immigrants to the United States during the nineteenth and twentieth centuries. But when the immigration is coerced—when, in effect, the subculture population is captured for importation—considerable dissidence and alienation may remain among its members; this has been the case among black Americans, whose ancestors were largely brought to North America involuntarily as slaves.

However it is fashioned, a subculture may face a bleak and precarious existence. It often consists of linguistic, racial, religious, or economic groups distinctively different from the elements of the dominant culture; the differences can provoke hostility, rejection, and suppression from controlling groups within a political system. Quite often, some form of deprivation is keenly experienced by members of the subculture. Indeed, the political alienation, nationalist impulses, and other political outlooks that set a subculture at odds with the dominant culture often result from prior social discrimination. Political resistance to the dominant cultural elements, once provoked, tends to incite further animosity toward the subculture, and a vicious circle of social and political alienation can erect further psychological barriers between the different cultural groupings. Sometimes, subcultural elements are gradually assimilated into the dominant culture through intermarriage, a relaxation of discrimination, the slow erosion of cultural identity, or other peaceful processes. Perhaps a *détente* can be negotiated between dominant and subordinate cultures, in which a measure of political autonomy is permitted the subcultures, or arrangements are made to incorporate them into the dominant political processes by various political formulas permitting representation in important political institutions. Such arrangements have worked reasonably well between Protestant and Catholic communities in Belgium, and among the numerous cultural groupings of Indonesia and Lebanon. When sub-cultures are tolerated, the cost is often a lingering anxiety, often verging on political paranoia among the subculture members, who may acutely feel their minority status and vulnerability to the will of the controlling political factions. In many political systems, subcultures have been forcibly eliminated by murder, extreme repression, or ostracism; this was the experience of numerous Jewish communities in Europe during the Nazi era, when Hitler's government practiced official genocide—the most vicious form of subcultural repression still found, in various forms, within some nations.

Regardless of how they are treated, subcultures that remain within political systems and cling to their uniqueness constitute a potential irritant, threat, or implicit challenge to the regime. Although instances can be found of subcultures existing in harmony with dominant national regimes, the accommodation between majority and minority—if it occurs—is likely to be fragile.

Disruptive Socialization

Few situations are more likely to create stress within a political culture than the socialization of the young into political outlooks hostile to a society's traditional political culture; sharp generational cleavages over basic political orientations can subvert an established political culture and introduce prolonged civil disorder within a nation. This situation, which we have called "disruptive socialization," until recently seemed confined to developing nations or to older states suddenly subjected to foreign occupation, internal revolution, or other events likely to create substantial differences in political values. Integrated political cultures seemed largely immune to such disruptive socialization; they were stable, in good part, because political socialization customarily indoctrinated the young into political outlooks compatible with existing cultural orientations.

The outbreak of widespread political protest and violence among American college students in the 1960's, part of a worldwide surge of political protest among college youth, seemed to throw such assumptions into considerable doubt. The United

States, presumably a very integrated political culture, had apparently produced a multitude of angry, alienated young people, highly dubious about their nation's virtues and behaving as if American political socialization, long producing millions of allegiant youth, had badly miscarried. More importantly, it seemed that disruptive socialization, far from remaining confined to developing countries, might occur in any system. Looking back, it appears that the intensity and durability of student alienation were exaggerated, and that pessimistic verdicts about American socialization's "failure" were premature. Still, a brief study of the causes and consequences of this dissent can be illuminating, for some generational conflicts and tensions were apparently genuine, and an understanding of their nature will provide some insight into factors which are able to produce disruptive socialization in integrated cultures.

A Familiar Issue, an Unfamiliar Setting. Culture stress does not inevitably flow from disruptive socialization, but the progression is likely. Such socialization induces or aggravates generational conflicts, can stimulate high levels of political violence between groups espousing antagonistic "old" and "new" values, and may hasten political polarization between social groups by reducing their shared orientations; ultimately, disruptive socialization may threaten national regimes, whose authority rests upon the dominant culture values challenged by the newer outlooks. If a large mass, or a strategic social group crucial to government, is influenced by this negative socialization, a psychology of crisis can develop within a society. Almost all major political conflicts and important policy decisions will be caught up in the tension between traditional and new culture, a high degree of real or imagined threat will be implicit in the conduct of politics, and widespread civic anxiety may persist for long periods.

Disruptive socialization has been most frequently observed in the developing nations.[9] Commonly, a modernizing elite, having gained control of a postcolonial country in the name of democracy, modernization, and independence, has looked upon the schools to equip the population for its new tasks. The youngest portion of the population were often taught technical skills appropriate to an industrialized economy, together with an appre-

ciation for the values and life styles associated with modernization. They were indoctrinated into accepting the concept of a
nation-state, taught the importance of bureaucratic organization
in public and private life, and told of the value of their citizenship. Moreover, they often came to expect basic civic rights, including voting, freedom of expression, and the right to join and
organize competitive political parties. They expected national
government to run more or less "democratically." But when these
carriers of a new culture emerged at different levels from the
educational system, they found an older generation often hostile
to such outlooks and unwilling to yield authority to the "modern"
generation. In politics, leaders often seemed less enthusiastic
about democracy than they had expected. In the economy, jobs
for the newly skilled were either unavailable or secured for older
workers. Modern administrative procedures were often widely
subverted in public and private institutions. Especially in the first
decades of national development, this collision between newer
and older life styles quickly triggered widespread civic disorder.

From this perspective, campus disorders in the United States
occurred in the wrong nation among the wrong individuals.
There were no massive cultural discontinuities separating an historically modern younger generation from a traditional older one,
as happened in the newer nations. There was no internal revolution, no sudden change in the content of official political socialization. The American school system had been producing millions
of allegiant youth for decades; a sudden radicalization of the
process seemed unthinkable. American youth were the wrong
people to have absorbed so many dissenting ideas. While it was
plausible for educationally and economically disadvantaged
youth—blacks, Chicanos, and American Indians among them—to
be alienated from the society, the inspirers and organizers of most
of the dissent were the sons and daughters of the American
middle and upper classes, attending the nation's better colleges.
The children of affluence, recipients of the nation's most coveted
rewards, had apparently turned upon their inheritance.

Dissent or Revolution? Student protest was not a uniquely
American experience in the mid-1960's. That decade saw worldwide student political activism, violence, and dissent arising so

generally that many observers suspected that a global generational cleavage might be appearing. In Great Britain, student
protesters closed the London School of Economics temporarily in
1967. In France, extensive student violence during May, 1968,
closed the Sorbonne and the university at Nanterre; the disruption
became so intense it appeared to approach civil war in several
Parisian student ghettos. Other outbreaks of street violence shut
the universities of Bonn and Berlin; in Italy and Japan, where
student violence had been traditional since the 1950's, the events
elsewhere incited new student activism.

In many respects, the cause of this student activism outside the
United States bore little resemblance to the American situation.
In Japan and France, for instance, universities were miserably
overcrowded, and classroom conditions frequently abominable
beyond anything American students encountered; this undoubtedly contributed much to the intensity of the protest. In Japan,
France, and Germany students were given virtually no voice in
any university functions; in Italy, political protest had been a
campus style for generations. In Europe and Asia, national governments had quite often failed to give universities the financial
support required to meet the escalating demands of a burgeoning
student population. However, the American protests did seem to
embody, with unusual clarity, a number of themes which could
also be found, in varying degree, among the student protests elsewhere; at the same time, there were unique elements in the
American experience.

American student protest, stretching across a decade and embracing a multitude of issues, never achieved an ideological
coherence. Beginning in the early 1960's as an outbreak of issue-
oriented protests, it gradually coalesced during the decade into
a mood of vehement criticism, if not rejection, of the American
"system."[10] A common theme, uniting otherwise disparate elements of the movement, was a widespread conviction of injustice
in American society. The movement started with the civil rights
crusades of the early 1960's, peaceful but impatient with traditional protest methods and favoring "direct action" and "civil disobedience." With the Indo-China War's intensification in the
mid-1960's and the advent of large draft calls, war protest and

civil rights movements often merged. In the later 1960's, the movement gained additional momentum from campus dissent against real and alleged suppression of student rights. With the assassinations of Martin Luther King, Jr., and Robert Kennedy in the late 1960's, the movement seemed to move toward an ever more critical examination and rejection of most American social and political institutions. It was this widening, deepening hostility toward fundamental social values which seemed to be the most menacing aspect of the movement.

But was this (as many commentators warned dramatically) a "revolution" in student values, with all the term implies about generational estrangement from traditional American civic culture? Apparently, the movement was far from a "revolution" involving mutually hostile cultural orientations, but it was symptomatic of a youthful disillusion with American political practice, and might, if continued long and reinforced with growing numbers of young people, produce serious civic disorders.

To put the movement in proper perspective, the protests involved only a comparatively few activists and supporters, on a restricted number of campuses, even at the height of dissent. "Even at the colleges that gathered together the greatest number of dissenters," writes one knowledgeable observer, "the vast majority of students—generally well over 95 per cent—remained interested onlookers or opponents rather than active dissenters;" most of the nation's 2,200 campuses were stirred but faintly, or largely unmoved, by the backwash of the most publicized demonstrations.[11] At the same time, the movement did generate enough student activism and sympathy—often passive—to suggest its attractiveness to many young people. By 1968, almost half the American college campuses had some student protest groups active, and roughly two-fifths of the college students polled by *Fortune* magazine in the late 1960's expressed sympathy for the viewpoints promulgated by the movement's leaders. At a time when half the country's college-age youth were on the campuses, and when the nation recruited its social elite from this group, even a minority commitment to radical values might have profound consequences.

There were also long-range consequences to consider. When

protest first spread, it was impossible to predict the durability of dissident opinions; collegiate values and life styles often fade after graduation. In the mid-1970's, however, it appeared that some of the disillusion and dissent had not only endured but had spread to non-college youth. According to a poll of American young people between the ages of sixteen and twenty-five conducted in the mid-1970's, the "new values" expressed by the student minority in the late 1960's had now become a majority viewpoint. "The New Values are now widely diffused throughout the total college population and are no longer confined to a minority," it reported. At the same time, "the single most striking finding of the study is the extent to which the gap in values between college and non-college youth has closed . . . non-college youth today are just about where the college population was in 1969."[12] Among the political opinions shared by youth, the poll found a large majority believing that the society was "democratic in name only," that "special interests ran the political machinery of the country," and that patriotism was "no longer a very important value."[13]

Nonetheless, were these "revolutionary" outlooks? Apparently, most of the youthful dissenters of the 1960's and 1970's had deeply embraced the dominant official values of the political system; they were rallying to the defense of free speech, public political participation, equality of political opportunity, and other commonly extolled American values. Essentially, there was an optimistic cast to much of this dissent in that it affirmed a belief in the values of political activism and the possibilities of change. The provocation to vigorous dissent and criticism of American institutions appeared to be a belief that the society had *failed* to accomplish its political and social objectives; it was not American cultural values, but their uneven realization, that lay at the root of student unrest. According to one study of student demonstrations, "demonstrators were 'acting out' in their demonstrations the values which their parents explicitly believed but did not have the courage or opportunity to practice or fight for."[14] While many studies affirmed the existence of a truly alienated group of young people, on campus and off, who rejected almost all American political values, these were a relatively small portion of students and other young people, who customarily retreated into private concerns and the "counterculture" without taking any significant part in political movements.

Even though student protest could not be traced to an alienation from basic American values—and, hence, could not be attributed to disruptive socialization as it is usually understood—it had the capacity to produce many of the same consequences as disruptive socialization: generational tensions, protests against established political authority and institutional behavior, and so forth. In this light, observers were interested in understanding the combination of factors producing the dissent, for it was reasonable to assume that analogous movements might arise in "advanced" nations again. A number of factors seemed to be associated with this type of militant dissidence:

1. *A large pool of affluent, educated, economically secure young people "available" for political action.* Many observers have suggested that this large number of students available for political mobilization will be characteristic of most industrialized, advanced nations in the future. According to this logic, American college youth were economically secure, unworried about future employment, had already savored the economic rewards of the society; they had the time and interest for political activism on a scale unmatched in most previous eras in American history. Moreover, they were sufficiently well educated to understand the news, distill from it historical trends, and associate them with themselves. In short, world historical forces are providing, in the advanced nations, a new, youthful political clientele for activism.

2. *A rising level of political expectations.* Young people are increasingly motivated by the discovery that the political system in which they live often fails to achieve its stated objectives. There is a growing impatience with this situation, an indication that American youth—and, perhaps, youth in most modern societies—are influenced by a wave of rising expectations for political system performance.

3. *The protest-promoting environment of the campus.* Many observers have suggested that the American college campus is an

unusually congenial environment for modern young people to learn to translate their political values into political activism. The colleges tend to recruit "protest-prone" students—intelligent, academically successful, liberal young people—and to concentrate them into a campus community, where strong group identifications grow and a consciousness of common interest intensifies. Further, college faculties often encourage dissent and protest, however unwittingly, by promoting critical thinking as a model behavior and by praising independence (or at least unconventionality) in behavior.

4. *A political culture stressing democratic norms and equality of political and economic opportunities.* American political culture, it has been asserted, is unusual in the extent to which it insists upon official norms that assume a high level of equality in social and political life. These values—even when very imperfectly realized—are a constant incentive to dissent and protest, particularly when the other conditions mentioned are also present.

It is, of course, far too early to render a final judgment about the validity of these arguments. What seems most apparent from the student protests of the 1960's is that Americans can no longer assume that their traditional methods of political socialization will guarantee a largely allegiant, uncritical, overwhelmingly supportive generation of young people in the future, and that other modern nations might be viewing, in the American experience, their own futures as well.

THE TRANSFER OF POLITICAL FORMS

For more than seventy years, the world has been witnessing a massive effort by the leading nations to transplant their national governmental institutions and values to other systems. Into this task have been poured enormous material resources, massive economic and political effort, and military and scientific manpower. Among the nations aggressively "exporting" their national political forms, this attempt to transfer political structures has assumed all the proportions of ideological competition. National pride, international prestige, and military and political advantage are presumed to be at stake; wars have been triggered, sustained, or extinguished according to the success or failure of such endeavors. It is appropriate to conclude a study of world political culture with a discussion of this phenomenon, one of the most audacious efforts at social engineering, whose outcome often depends upon the ability of one government to remake the political culture of another.

It is understandable that political culture should become a crucial consideration in the transfer of political forms. We have seen that the nature of citizen orientations to national political institutions is always a major—if not *the* major—factor in determining whether such institutions prosper. For the student of political culture, the most salient questions concern the nature of the transfers attempted—that is, what forms are being "grafted"—and the conditions that facilitate or frustrate such efforts.

Three Variations on Cultural Imperialism. Imposing a new political system upon a people, under whatever circumstances, has become a form of cultural imperialism. The object—not always acknowledged explicitly—is for one nation to bring another within its power ambit, tightening the bonds of alliance by reducing the ideological and institutional dissimilarities between the peoples involved. Cultural imperialism is a great-power game. The smaller powers (not necessarily in population or area but in political and military might) are the pawns, however unwillingly; the target populations are likely to be the "developing nations," the losers in major wars, and the smaller nations with inherently fragmented political cultures, that is, all the countries made vulnerable to cultural imperialism by circumstance.

Today, this cultural imperialism can be observed in three different, but often associated, forms. To begin, there is the effort to *modernize* the underdeveloped nations by exporting to them the economic, social, and political institutions most often associated with the advanced nations. We have seen that, politically, this involves the creation of a nation-state with a sovereign national government, the erection of a modern governmental administrative apparatus staffed with skilled bureaucrats, the development of a representative legislative body, and the endow-

ment of the regime with generous powers enabling it to penetrate
all important segments of society. This is frequently accompanied
by the window dressing of democracy.

Out of the competitive ideological struggle between the Soviet
Union and the United States have grown campaigns to either
Americanize or *Sovietize* large portions of the world—a bipolar
exercise in competitive cultural exportation, which both sides
assert to be in the cause of democracy.

The campaign to Americanize the world has involved a loudly
proclaimed intention by the United States to protect democracy
where it presently exists and to promote it where it does not
flourish. Officially, American statesmen have tended to equate
democracy with political institutions found in the United States—
particularly mass parties, interparty competition, and popularly
elected public officials—and to talk as if democratizing the world
were a moral crusade for which the United States had been particularly anointed. As a practical matter, however, American statesmen have been quite selective concerning where and how they
crusaded. In the immediate aftermath of World War II, the United
States felt an obligation to use its occupation of Japan, West
Germany, and Italy as an opportunity to implant democratic
values and institutions where non-democratic forms had previously existed. But during the Indo-China War, American policy-
makers, having turned South Vietnam into a clientele state,
seemed content with a rather superficial "democratization" of the
country in which democratic forms were instituted with American pressure but actual democracy seemed weak; in other parts
of the world, such as Europe, the United States seemed quite
willing to form close alliances with nations, such as Spain and
Portugal, which made no pretense of democracy. All of which
suggests that the United States has had a rather ambivalent attitude toward democracy in other states: it may claim an ideological commitment to democratizing the world, but it has been willing to collaborate with non-democratic regimes when it seemed
useful in the game of world power politics.

The Soviet Union, regarding itself as the chief exponent and
interpreter of worldwide Marxism, has inspired, underwritten,
and trained the leaders of "national liberation movements" in

non-Communist countries. Immediately following the end of World War II, the Soviet Union absorbed into its own sphere all the European nations immediately along its western border, converting them into satellite states organized and functioning along distinctly Soviet lines. Shortly thereafter, mainland China fell to insurgent Communist forces. The Soviets continue to encourage "wars of national liberation" in all non-Communist systems. A few states (such as Yugoslavia) have managed to maintain great independence from Soviet manipulation while remaining in the Communist bloc, and others (such as China) have gradually drifted away from close collaboration with Moscow, but the majority of Communist bloc countries are, apparently, heavily influenced in governmental structure and policy by Moscow. Indeed, so relentlessly have Soviet leaders insisted that most Communist bloc nations follow Soviet cues on matters of international and domestic policy that many observers believe Moscow's campaign to export worldwide Communism smacks as much of Russian chauvinism as it does of pure Marxist class revolution.

The United States and the Soviet Union have both experienced mixed results in their competitive struggle. The United States has apparently been successful in nurturing democratic political processes in West Germany, Japan, Italy, and India but has been less successful in South Vietnam and Taiwan. The Soviet Union has apparently succeeded in implanting a Soviet-type system in most Eastern European countries, in Cuba, and in North Vietnam, but its dominance in Czechoslovakia and Poland seems shaky (although the extent of actual resistance to Sovietization is difficult to determine). Many of the postcolonial nations have desperately attempted to avoid being reduced to satellites of either major power by a policy of "nonalignment" involving a very delicate and dangerous game of playing one major power against the other while taking advantage of some of the resources and influence of each. It is, however, a case of riding the back of the tiger for the smaller states; "nonalignment" always places them in a precarious position, for both major powers are constantly tempted to intervene in the internal affairs of the country when a threat to their own interests arises.

When Prospects Are Promising. There are a number of circumstances that seem congenial to the transfer of political forms from one system to another. Because there are many exceptions and qualifications, any enumeration of these promising circumstances must be considered very tentative. Still, they are suggestive.

First, *the transfer of political forms seems most successful when an incumbent national regime has lost its sovereignty, its coercive resources, and its widespread popular allegiance.* Such a situation is most likely to arise from the loss of a major war, from the rapid withdrawal of an occupying power (such as a colonial regime vacating a country), or from an inability to manage an internal crisis of such proportions that the society is gravely disrupted and most civic and economic life cannot be conducted normally. Especially at the conclusion of a disastrous war, or at the end of a prolonged social crisis of major proportions, public confidence in regime leaders and institutions is likely to be tenuous, the regime's credibility badly reduced; it may seem to the public that the political formula used to govern the nation has, itself, failed. This is not to suggest that a significantly new political system will emerge within a nation under such circumstances, but the nation is clearly vulnerable to such a change.

Second, *the presence of military occupation forces representing the new regime* almost always accompanies a radical change in national political forms. It is noteworthy that the most successful efforts of both the Soviet Union and the United States to transfer their political forms—in Eastern Europe (for the Soviets) and in defeated Germany and Japan (for the United States)—were accompanied by the military occupation of those countries. It is also true that civil wars, apparently arising from largely domestic issues, may topple one regime and lead to another, but today these civil wars are rarely conducted without major political and material help from an outside power, usually a major one; indeed, the help may amount to the outside power's sending trained guerilla fighters or other revolutionaries into the troubled nation to such an extent that the outside power is, in effect, providing part of the army that will protect the new regime if it successfully performs a coup.

Finally, *the transfer of forms seems to work best when the new regime takes immediate control of the political socialization pro-*

cess and operates it for several decades. A new regime, especially, needs to bring the younger citizen generations within its secure influence almost immediately to ensure that it will enjoy a solid foundation of support over time. A transfer of forms seems to require that this manipulation of basic political learning among the young be controlled as directly as possible by the new regime, or by the outside power sponsoring the regime change. In the case of the Weimar Republic (1920–32), a democratic system strongly supported by the victorious Allies after Germany's defeat in World War I collapsed into fascism. One major cause appears to have been a failure of the Allied powers and the leaders of the Weimar government to control the socialization of German youth during the critical decade following the creation of the new system.

All this is not to suggest that major regime transformations will occur within a polity only under these conditions and with the active participation of an outside, usually major, power. But the majority of cases in the modern world in which regime transfers have occurred have apparently been under circumstances resembling these.

Are Some Forms More Exportable than Others? A scholar once warned Americans overzealous to democratize the world that democracy was not a piece of plumbing that could be installed in any nation's household. In light of the massive resources now being poured into the competition between major powers to export their political forms, one can appropriately wonder which forms, if any, travel best.

In cases where the major national exporter of a political system has an opportunity to impose its new regime on another nation at bayonet point—the customary case in occupied countries after World War II—it appears that almost any major political form can be rooted firmly in a national culture; what is needed is sufficient time, coercive ability, and dedication to the task by the major power. Such a conclusion, however, ignores the fact that the Soviet Union has never permitted open, competitive elections in any satellite state where its own system now prevails over a previously existing national political culture. If political freedom was suddenly restored to the Sovietized states—that is, if they ceased to be Sovietized long enough for open popular elections—

the durability of the Soviet political forms might prove problematic. At the moment, however, there is no reason to believe that the political cultures in the Soviet satellite states are so inhospitable to Soviet forms that a major rejection of the new order will occur.

In most of the newer states, it does not appear that a liberal democratic political form is likely to prosper; indeed, in many, the democratic institutions created at the time of national independence have decayed into autocracy. Highly undemocratic, illiberal political regimes prevail. This certainly suggests that the prognosis for democratic political forms patterned after the American example—such institutions as competitive political parties, popularly elected legislators and executives, generous political liberties, and much else—is not promising. It does not follow, however, that highly autocratic political forms patterned after the Soviet system are likely to be more popular. Rather, it appears that many of the developing nations are likely to opt for relatively autocratic political systems—albeit not necessarily Soviet in form or philosophy—in which the central government rigidly limits political liberties and democracy is often reduced to a charade. In short, outside of Western Europe and Japan, democracy has not traveled very well.

Why have democratic forms been more difficult to transplant to the newer nations than less democratic forms? Some scholars have argued that true democracy requires a high degree of citizen education, a relatively affluent society with a broad base of common cultural orientations, a cultural inheritance of democratically inspired law, and other circumstances wholly unlike those confronting most of the newer nations. Democracy, according to this reasoning, does not thrive in most new nations, because the socio-economic settings are not congenial—indeed, some observers believe that the national settings in which democracy can prosper are so relatively limited that it is foolish to expect most peoples of the world to embrace such a system. If this reasoning is accurate, the many hybrids of authoritarian or totalitarian systems are more likely to dominate among the world's political cultures.

NOTES

1. A useful survey of the education and socialization of native elites may be found in James S. Coleman (ed.), *Education and Political Development* (Princeton, N.J.: Princeton University Press, 1965), Part III: "The Education of Modern Elites in Developing Countries."
2. Edward Shils, *Political Development in the New States* (The Hague: Mouton, 1966), p. 19.
3. On patterns of decay in postcolonial democratic systems, see *ibid.*, chapter 3.
4. Herbert McClosky, "Consensus and Ideology in American Politics," *American Political Science Review* 58 (June, 1964), 361–82.
5. *Ibid.*
6. Two such critiques are Robert W. Jackman, "Political Elites, Mass Publics and Support for Democratic Principles." *Journal of Politics*, 34 (August, 1972), 753–73; and Jack Walker, "A Critique of the Elitist Theory of Democracy," *American Political Science Review*, 60 (June, 1966), 285–95.
7. On the Southern culture generally, see W. J. Cash, *The Mind of the South* (New York: Alfred A. Knopf, 1941).
8. On black political culture generally, see Joel D. Aberbach and Jack L. Walker, *Race in the City* (Boston: Little, Brown, 1973), chapter 6.
9. The "discontinuities" in political socialization are usefully summarized and explored in Richard E. Dawson and Kenneth Prewitt, *Political Socialization* (Boston: Little, Brown, 1969), chapter 6.
10. The development of this student protest is perceptively described in Joseph A. Califano, Jr., *The Student Revolution* (New York: W. W. Norton, 1970).
11. Kenneth Keniston, "The Sources of Student Dissent," *Journal of Social Issues*, 23 (June, 1967).
12. *New York Times*, May 26, 1974.
13. *Ibid.*
14. Keniston, *op. cit.*, p. 233.

BIBLIOGRAPHY

ADAMS, JOHN CLARKE, and PAOLO BARILE. *The Government of Republican Italy.* Boston: Houghton-Mifflin, 1966.

AKE, CLAUDE. *A Theory of Political Integration.* Homewood, Ill.: Dorsey Press, 1967.

ALMOND, GABRIEL, and JAMES S. COLEMAN (eds.). *The Politics of the Developing Areas.* Princeton, N.J.: Princeton University Press, 1960.

ALMOND, GABRIEL, and C. BINGHAM POWELL. *Comparative Politics: A Developmental Approach.* Boston: Little, Brown, 1966.

ALMOND, GABRIEL, and SIDNEY VERBA. *The Civic Culture.* Princeton, N.J.: Princeton University Press, 1963.

ANDERSON, CHARLES W.; FRED R. VON DER MEHDEN; and CRAWFORD YOUNG. *Issues of Political Development.* Englewood Cliffs, N.J.: Prentice-Hall, 1967.

BANFIELD, EDWARD C. *The Moral Basis of a Backward Society.* Glencoe, Ill.: Free Press, 1965.

BEER, SAMUEL H. *British Politics in the Collectivist Age.* New York: Alfred A. Knopf, 1965.

BLACK, C. E. *The Dynamics of Modernization.* New York: Harper & Row, 1966.

BLONDELL, JEAN, and GODFREY DREXEL, JR. *The Government of France.* New York: Thomas Y. Crowell, 1968.

COLEMAN, JAMES S. (ed.). *Education and Political Development.* Princeton, N.J.: Princeton University Press, 1965.

DAWSON, RICHARD E., and KENNETH PREWITT. *Political Socialization.* Boston: Little, Brown, 1968.

DEUTSCH, KARL W., and WILLIAM F. FOLTZ (eds.). *Nation Building.* New York: Atherton Press, 1963.

DEVINE, DONALD J. *The Political Culture of the United States.* Boston: Little, Brown, 1972.

ECKSTEIN, HARRY (ed.). *Internal War.* New York: Free Press, 1964.

ERICKSON, ROBERT S., and NORMAN LUTTBEG. *American Public Opinion.* New York: John Wiley, 1973.

GEERTZ, CLIFFORD (ed.). *Old Societies and New States.* New York: Free Press, 1963.

HESS, ROBERT D., and JUDITH TORNEY. *The Development of Political Attitudes in Children.* Chicago: Aldine Press, 1967.

HOLT, ROBERT D., and JOHN E. TURNER (eds.). *The Methodology of Comparative Research.* New York: Free Press, 1970.

LANE, ROBERT E., and DAVID O. SEARS. *Public Opinion.* Englewood Cliffs, N.J.: Prentice-Hall, 1964.

LAPALOMBARA, JOSEPH. *Interest Groups in Italian Politics.* Princeton, N.J.: Princeton University Press, 1964.

LIPSET, SEYMOUR M. *The First New Nation.* New York: Basic Books, 1963.

MILBRATH, LESTER. *Political Participation.* Chicago: Rand, McNally, 1965.

OLORUNSOLA, VICTOR A. (ed.). *The Politics of Cultural Sub-Nationalism in Africa.* Garden City, N.Y.: Anchor Books, 1972.

PRZEWORSKI, ADAM, and HENRY TEUNE. *The Logic of Comparative Social Inquiry.* New York: John Wiley, 1970.

PYE, LUCIEN. *Aspects of Political Development.* Boston: Little, Brown, 1966.

PYE, LUCIEN, and SIDNEY VERBA (eds.). *Political Culture and Political Development.* Princeton, N.J.: Princeton University Press, 1965.

ROSE, RICHARD. *England.* Boston: Little, Brown, 1964.

————. *Governing Without Consensus.* Boston: Beacon Press, 1971.

RUBIN, LESLIE, and BRIAN WEINSTEIN. *Introduction to African Politics: A Continental Approach.* New York: Praeger Publishers, 1974.

SIGEL, ROBERTA (ed.). *Learning About Politics: Studies in Political Socialization.* New York: Random House, 1973.

VERBA, SIDNEY, and NORMAN NIE. *Political Participation.* New York: Harper & Row, 1973.

WEISSBERG, ROBERT. *Political Learning.* Englewood Cliffs, N.J.: Prentice-Hall, 1974.

YOUNG, CRAWFORD. *Politics in the Congo.* Princeton, N.J.: Princeton University Press, 1965.

ZARISKI, RAPHAEL. *Italy.* Hinsdale, Ill.: Dryden Press, 1972.

INDEX

The Author

WALTER A. ROSENBAUM is Associate Professor of Political Science at the University of Florida in Gainesville. He is the author of *The Politics of Environmental Concern* and has been a program analyst for the U.S. Environmental Protection Agency, researching the impact of the National Environmental Policy Act. Professor Rosenbaum received his doctorate from Princeton University. He has contributed numerous articles to professional journals and is a co-author of *Analyzing American Politics* and co-editor of *Political Opinion and Behavior.*